ROCK
THE
CRADLE

by

MARIE PANETH

2ND GENERATION
PUBLISHING

Second Generation Publishing Company
355 Wilmslow Road
Fallowfield
Manchester M14 6XU

©2020 Library of Congress, Washington, D.C.
Marie Paneth Papers, Sigmund Freud Collection, Manuscript Division, Library of Congress, Washington, D.C.

Cover design Miroslaw Balka
Photograph taken in Spain at 7.58 am on 22 April 2020, looking in the direction of Tel Aviv

Compiled and arranged by Trevor Avery BEM, Director of LDHP

First published in the UK by Second Generation Publishing Company in 2020.

By kind permission of the family of Marie Paneth

ISBN 978-1-84547-274-0 (Pbk)
ISBN 978-1-84547-275-7 (Hbk)

Acknowledgements

There are many people and contacts who deserve a special mention, and in many instances much more than a thank you, for working with us and offering advice, guidance, and not a little enthusiast support for the work of 2nd Generation Publishing and Lake District Holocaust Project. Without their support, past and present, the publication of this book would not have been possible.

Thanks to the family of Marie Paneth, and especially Penny Paneth and Tom Ulrich, for their enthusiasm, engagement, and their kind permission that has enabled us to publish the book. Also thanks to Dr Margaret McAleer at the US Library of Congress for support and guidance. Others that deserve a mention include the daughter of one of our very own Windermere Girls, Cathy Edmunds, who helped enormously in editing and in providing further enthusiastic endorsement of our ambitions to have it finally published after so many years, and to my colleague Rosemary Smith who really pulled the edit together and carried out so much work on it. Thanks to Kanta Walker for the initial transcribing. Thanks also to Arts Council England and to National Lottery Heritage Fund, and to Nancy and Ben at Wall to Wall, who saw the importance of what we had discovered immediately. Thanks to Sir Ben Helfgott, Angela Cohen and 45 Aid Society for their guidance and for listening and for their encouragement over the years; to Romola Garai who portrayed Marie so perfectly in *The Windermere Children*; to Miroslaw Balka for providing a design for the book; to Sir Peter Bazelguette, Sir Nicholas Serota, Tim Kiddell, and to so many others associated with everything that grew from the Prime Minister's Holocaust Commission of 2015. To Eleanor Greene, Leanne Klein, Nancy Bornat, Simon Block (screenwriter *The Windermere Children*), and all at Wall to Wall, to the BBC, and to Tim Rostock and Warner Bros for the magnificent appearance of *The Windermere Children* and *The Windermere Children – In Their Own Words* in 2020.

A very special mention to all the former residents of Calgarth Estate, a unique place and a unique wartime community that showed Britain at its best.

And finally, to all the 45 Aid Society survivors and their families especially Ike Alterman, Sir Ben Helfgott, Arek Hersh, Sam Laskier, Harry Olmer, whose personal appearances in The Windermere Children touched people around the world...Thank You.

2nd Generation Publishing and Lake District Holocaust Project

Central British Fund and World Jewish Relief

The Jewish children who were brought to the Lake District in the summer of 1945 were the first group of a final total of 732 young Holocaust survivors who came to Britain after the war through the remarkable work of Central British Fund, now known as World Jewish Relief. Marie Paneth was one of a number of people from so many walks of life that were brought together by CBF to help in the recovery and rehabilitation of children and young people who had suffered unimaginably during the Holocaust. The children arrived at Windermere and subsequently other locations in the UK including Southampton, Glasgow and Northern Ireland, having lost so much. There were people on hand to help them in the immediate days after their liberation and for some considerable time afterwards. *Rock the Cradle* offers a unique glimpse into the world of the carer at the front line in providing help. However, this book is not simply a historic journal from a different time. It holds lessons for the present day and for the future. The work of World Jewish Relief, 45 Aid Society, and all organisations and individuals involved in humanitarian work, provide the essential counter balance to cruelty, hatred, and impoverishment. If the publication of this book shines a light on the extraordinary goodness at work and delivered by compassionate, caring individuals operating at the front line of pain and suffering, then it will have served its purpose. And the legacy of Marie Paneth, and all those who offer help like her, will act as an inspiration to those who follow in her footsteps.

Contents

Foreword   5

Introduction   11

Part 1 - The Arrival   13

Part 2 - The Survivors   43

Part 3 - The Struggle   105

Part 4 - The Windermere Children   119

Foreword

Marie Paneth was one of a team of carers that was assembled in the Lake District by the Central British Fund during August of 1945. She had arrived a few days previously to help prepare for the scheduled arrival of a large group of young Jewish survivors from the concentration camps, and to ensure that all was ready for what was considered to be a step into the unknown for all concerned. The situation that was facing the carers was unprecedented...

Rock the Cradle is her remarkable description of that very moment, written both at the time and in her own words

Freedom had arrived for the young survivors in the springtime but the challenges of the future still lay ahead. When they arrived in the middle of the idyllic Lake District in the summer of 1945 they were to describe it as if arriving in Paradise, and Marie was one of those there to care for them. This book is her eye witness account of those moments, and follows her on her journey with a small group of the survivors after they had moved on to new pastures.

What is remarkable about Marie's appearance in the acclaimed BBC drama *The Windermere Children*, is that she was not even mentioned in the earlier versions of the script treatment. The sudden discovery and revelations contained within her unpublished book *Rock the Cradle*, which came to light late in the development of the film, was so compelling that it was very clear she had to be included on screen.

The book showed that not only had Marie composed the book based on notes taken at the time, but that she had also, very soon afterwards, reflected on her experiences in the Lake District and for a while afterwards. What the book revealed was a personal and contemporary eye witness account of a remarkable moment in time, and for this alone it is invaluable and unique.

The book should not be seen as the definitive description of the Windermere Reception Camp. It adds a specific colour to the children who stayed there, and to the locality and community who were living there at the time. She is often at pains to stress that much of her comments are based on conjecture and offers an honest opinion of her limitations, but the book is none-the-less a hugely important document in its own right. Some of her descriptions of life on Windermere Reception Camp are vivid indeed, and recognisable to those of us who know the story thoroughly, while other perceptions that she offers are often thought provoking.

Certainly, for those of us who have been part of the Lake District Holocaust Project for so many years, Marie provided a unique insight into the connections that were established between the young survivors and the local community that lived around them on the estate.

This relationship has often been overlooked by commentators and researchers but not, significantly, by the child survivors themselves. When many of the survivors talk of their time spent in the Lake District, the landscape is revered and also the local community emerge warmly and are described as being 'good people in a good country'. The relationship between the children and the locals was not the result of any official policy or strategy; it was based on a groundswell of goodwill that extended towards the youngsters from those who met with them on Calgarth Estate, otherwise known to Marie as Windermere Reception Camp. There had been concerns about how the local community would react to the arrival of such a large group of young survivors of the concentration camps but, as Marie herself says, it went much better than they expected or hoped for.

So where do you begin to unravel the complex, interwoven threads that lie behind this publication of *Rock the Cradle* by Marie Paneth? Threads that include hard work, perseverance and not a little happenstance?

An old friend of mine in Ireland once said the telling of history depends on 'where you dig your well, and where you draw your water from'. That perceptive wisdom applies in this instance as well as any other.

So let me tell you of my part in *Rock the Cradle* in the hope that it will serve as a touchstone to this remarkable story.

For many years, I have been involved in the history of how 300 child Holocaust Survivors came to be in the Lake District of Wordsworth, Coleridge, and the Romantic poets. The children arrived in Cumbria a few weeks after their liberation at the end of the Second World War.

The transition proved a massive shock. Years later, Jack Aizenberg, one of the children, said 'the change of circumstance' from the concentration camps of Nazi Occupied Europe to the solitude of Windermere and the Lake District was astonishing.

I began to dedicate time to uncovering the story of the Jewish children and their links to the Lake District some 15 years before the publication of this book. It was still possible then to meet many of these remarkable youngsters in their later years.

Moreover, I was able to meet many of the local community who remained in the area, and who had lived on and around the place where the Jewish children stayed in 1945, namely the now 'lost' wartime village of Calgarth Estate.

The estate had been a Second World War workers' housing scheme that had been controversially embedded at the heart of the Lakes in the 1940s. It was once home to a thriving community of workers, and their families, all linked to the nearby Short's flying boat factory at White Cross Bay on the shores of Windermere.

Calgarth Estate was located at Troutbeck Bridge, not far from Windermere. Although the physical remainders of the estate have long gone, the stories of life on 'Cal-garth' live on in the folk memory of many former residents who still live nearby.

As the numbers of the survivors have steadily declined over the years, so has the number of local witnesses to life on the estate; witnesses who recalled the children arriving and staying amongst them. In hindsight, I was fortunate indeed to begin collecting memories and recollections at what was the right time, and just in time.

It is a story of a unique wartime community that welcomed the Jewish children 'into their hearts' as former aircraft worker Brian Crosland stated. It was a dramatic event for the Calgarth Estate residents when these traumatised, yet resilient, young Holocaust Survivors arrived to live amongst them in the former hostels on the estate. The war was over in the summer of 1945 but an aspect its dreadful legacy was brought close to home to the local people who had lived in this remote area for a number of years.

So just what was it that was so compelling about the story of these young people coming to live in the Lake District that drew me to it in the first place - a story that was little known at the time but has grown in stature and renown over the years?

Professor Tony Kushner once offered me an explanation: 'The story is so compelling because it is the coming together of two Epics - the Epic tragedy of the Holocaust coming into collision with the Epic sweep of the Romantic landscape of the Lake District'.

So, it was like two worlds colliding? In a way, yes, although I would also add that the intimate relationships that developed between many of these young survivors and their British working-class neighbours on the estate were just as compelling. In certain circumstances the meeting of these two communities was less a collision and more like a gentle coming together.

A short time before the Jewish children arrived, the local community that would welcome them had already witnessed the arrival of a self-conscious group of 'Offcomers', mainly from London but also from other towns and cities across the UK.

These 'Offcomers' (a term used locally to describe folks not from the area) formed a team of carers, support staff, and volunteers from Central British Fund (CBF, now World Jewish Relief) that had been brought together under the umbrella of a kindly philanthropist by the name of Leonard Montefiore. They were to be on the ground in the Lake District to welcome the Jewish children and to provide support and assistance on their arrival at Calgarth.

Amongst the psychiatrists, nurses, cooks and volunteers, there was one person who literally stood head and shoulders above her new colleagues.

Her name was Marie Paneth.

The New Yorker publication dated 29th April 1939 offers an insight into the physical characteristics that made Marie such a striking figure, and perhaps also offers a glimpse into her occasional expressions of personality.

"In writing of Dorothy Vicaji, the English portrait painter, we described her as the tallest woman painter in the world. Mrs. Marie Paneth, a Viennese artist, is six feet one – a clear inch and a half over Miss V. She lives and paints in a studio in Carnegie Hall. She has been there for five months, and her studio is filled with innumerable canvasses, pots of ivy, and a Chianti tree - her own somewhat surrealistic idea.

She's apt to concoct something like this when in a stormy mood. Another time, temporarily angry at New York, she painted Manhattan Island upside down, with flowers growing in Wall Street and only one inhabitant, a large baby llama. She has done skyscrapers, Harlem Lindy hoppers, and Fulton St. Fish Market".

It is hard to say how much of this piece of satire we can take seriously, but we can agree that Marie Paneth had something of a presence in New York society.

She was born in Sukdull, near Wurzing, in Austria on 15th August 1895 and we know that she was an artist, painter and pedagogue.

Her father, Alfred Furth, came from a family that owned a large fez factory in Strakoniz in Bohemia, although he was not wealthy. He left his wife, Marie Jeiteles, and four young children – Walter, Marie, Hans Johann and Gertrude – with no visible means of support when he died in 1899 at the age of 40. It was only the generosity of her mother's Jewish family, one of the most prominent in Bohemia, that sustained Marie and her siblings.

Marie studied in Vienna and married Otto Paneth, a doctor, in June 1918. Otto was the son of the physiologist Joseph Paneth, who numbered Sigmund Freud among his friends. In turn, Marie came to know Freud herself in the years before she and Otto moved to the Dutch East Indies, now Indonesia.

Marie and Otto also worked in the USA and the Netherlands after the First World War, and had three children – Brigitte, Matthias and Anton. Their marriage broke down in the latter half of the 1930s and they were later divorced.

After returning to Europe, Marie worked in Paris and arrived in New York in 1938. She developed a close relationship with one of Freud's pupils, the psychoanalyst and psychiatrist Heinz Hartmann.

During her seven months in New York, Marie's work was exhibited in the 1939 Society of Independent Artists' annual show before she sailed for Southampton in July. She was listed as a 'female enemy alien' when she first came to the UK, but was classed as a non-refugee after a successful appeal. Described as an artist-painter, she worked as a matron at Gordonstoun School in Elgin, Scotland.

Marie then moved to London, living in Chelsea and Hampstead, and started to work with children in five London boroughs.

We know that she was deeply interested in working with traumatised children. Her involvement with children who had suffered in the London Blitz (the bombings on London and Britain that sought to break the spirit of its communities) was recorded in her book 'Branch Street'.

She practised the then infant discipline of Art Therapy when the term itself had barely come into common usage. Her interest in child-centred art can be traced to her studies in Vienna, years before under the artist Franz Cižek, himself a proponent of child-centred art and learning.

We can see how her reputation and successes with the children in London would confirm her as a positive asset when the personnel were identified to come and help in the care of the children coming from the concentration camps to the Lake District in August 1945. Marie Paneth became more than a consideration; she became an obvious choice.

Her involvement with the 'Windermere Reception Camp' would have remained something of a lost treasure had it not been for the reappearance of the original draft of *Rock the Cradle* in archives in the US. As we uncovered more and more information over the years, about the children themselves, about the estate, about the local context, then more questions arose about the mechanisms of the care and help that were on hand.

The focus for us all working on the project in the Lake District began to shift to accommodate some of the discoveries we uncovered that told of those carers who had been brought to the Lakes to look after the children. Conversations with interviewees and historical curators led to the name 'Marie Paneth' being mentioned as a member of the original team in Windermere. As with any good detective journey there were various leads that required following, and both my close colleague Rosemary Smith and myself were working on parallel lines, uncovering material at an exciting and tremendous rate. Rosemary led the way in contacting the US Library of Congress, liaising with them, and both she and I quickly realised what we had uncovered.

Although we had little awareness of what actually lay in store when we entered distant archives, the moment that the existence of the draft of *Rock the Cradle* came to light, along with other documents and files kept by Marie that were connected to Windermere and the survivor children, well, it was clear we had come across something extraordinary.

The draft book proved to be a revelation to us. We had collected many interviews and stories from the children themselves, and we had many further stories from the community that welcomed them, but *Rock the Cradle* provided the crucial link between these two disparate groups who lived on Calgarth Estate for six fascinating months in the second half of 1945.

Marie's observations about life on Calgarth Estate and the relationship she witnessed between the Jewish children and the local community was, for us, hugely significant. This alone would have been enough, but her descriptions of these deeply traumatised camp survivors at the very moment of their arrival, and her observations on their lives in those early days in Britain, were nothing short of an astounding discovery.

After thirteen years since first setting out on a journey that would change my life, *Rock the Cradle* appeared as if from nowhere.

I cannot end without saying a few words of huge gratitude and appreciation for the work of my friend and colleague Rosemary Smith, who really led the way on this remarkable discovery, as she has in so much work with Lake District Holocaust Project over the years. It is often said that achievements could not have happened without the help and support of someone in particular, and in this instance it is absolutely the case. Rosemary was, and remains, indispensable to the project.

My thanks also to the family of Marie Paneth who have helped us piece together fragments of her life and have granted permission for us to go ahead and publish this remarkable book, and to the US Library of Congress for being so helpful and positive throughout.

In many ways, Marie was an enigma and remains so to this day. But her contribution, and the contribution of all those who helped to care for those traumatised children who came to live amongst us for a short time in 1945, carers and the local community, deserves to be fully recognised. This book goes a little way towards doing just that.

As for those remarkable survivor children that Marie cared for in the Lake District? Eventually there was a final total of 732 youngsters who were brought to the UK under the same scheme that brought this first group to Windermere Reception Camp. They were to establish their own charitable and philanthropic organisation called the 45 Aid Society, which is still going strong today.

This astonishing episode in Lake District history that Marie writes about is a story that will continue to reverberate through the ages because Windermere Reception Camp was the beginning of a journey of recovery for these children, and it was a journey that would lead, in the words of the revered historian Sir Martin Gilbert, to the ultimate 'Triumph over Adversity'.

TREVOR AVERY BEM, DIRECTOR
LAKE DISTRICT HOLOCAUST PROJECT
JULY 2020

ROCK THE CRADLE

by Marie Paneth, 1947

Introduction

This book aims to serve the same purpose as a portrait; to enable those who read it to become familiar with the features of the portrayed. It is divided into three parts, each dealing with different sets of people. The first describes The Arrival of a large group. The second deals with The Intensive Work with a small group of Survivors. The third speaks of The Struggle of an individual.

What all three sets have in common are the experiences which preceded The Arrival, as well as the most striking features of the appearance of those portrayed. The sad case described in the third part shares these attributes, but has a different, more negative slant.

After the incidents described in The Arrival had taken place, I was initially reluctant to write about them. I looked upon the boys and girls as if they were behind a sheet of glass, and, at first, I wished them to stay that way; outside our community and outside our daily common lives, due to their uncommon experiences. I knew too much of their past and not enough, yet, of them as people, not to feel awed in their presence and unsure of my impressions. It was only while the intensive work of the second part was in progress, when I was permitted to give and share, and allowed myself to do so, that I found I could grasp their outlines and discover how utterly of us they were—if not more so, if you take us to mean warm-hearted, alive, natural, kind-hearted, keen, independent and, above all, realists. Then the sheet of glass disappeared, but I still would not have had the courage to write about them had it not been for the revelation of what learning had meant to our group. I felt compelled to communicate this, and so I reversed my earlier decision.

I have tried to describe some of their experiences here in order to give an overview of the work which was done by them, for them, and with them.

To do justice to my task, I have sometimes had to talk about the children's past. What they told me has been confirmed in both broad outline and finer detail by the adults who shared these experiences, but even if it is not all entirely accurate, I think there can be some leeway, as it is the therapy itself with which I am concerned. My attitude towards the children would be the same whether they had seen with their own eyes all the atrocities they talked about, or had witnessed only some, and imagined the rest; whether they were suffering from mental images of sadism or had experienced it all in reality and felt the full horror directly.

Whichever it was, they had still experienced the storms through which the ship of the young person must sail before reaching the high seas of adulthood.

We, who worked with them, found there were many factors which had equal importance in determining their current state of mental health and therefore had to be taken into account in any future prognosis. These included the age at which they were sent to the camps, and whether they had spent nearly six years there as in the case of the Poles, or three years for the Czechs, or only about one year for the Hungarians and Rusyns.

A life spent in concentration camps presents an accumulation of soul and body-destroying elements which add up every single day. Children cannot report back on this. They can only talk of the conditions under which they had to exist. Perhaps our imagination allows us to follow them and share, for a brief moment, something of the pain and degradation they had to suffer for years. It is impossible to communicate in words the enormity of what happened, and what was missed. The critical fact is that it went on for years. Language is an inadequate medium to express this fully. When it commands our attention, it can do no more than rush us through a series of brightly lit close-ups, and must always, by its very nature, miss out much of the bleak, underexposed, empty and endless stretches of exposures which seem to record almost nothing.

Another determining point, and to my mind the most important one, was the background of their childhood before the Nazi world destroyed it. Almost all the youngsters who came to England were from large families. Were they therefore more capable of 'taking it'? Were they better able to blend the 'good' past they had known with the thought of a bearable future, of allowing the wound slowly to close over a hurt which should never have happened, than the only child, with its lesser training in making compromise? Had their cradle been rocked, gently and wisely, in a rhythm which gave them security, and which they could reproduce again when they were free?

*NB According to recent discoveries in archives, the actual day of the children arriving in the UK was 14th August 1945.

Part 1

The Arrival

Seven hundred young people from German concentration camps were issued with permits from the Home Office, allowing them to enter Great Britain and to stay there until they could proceed further. This 'further' was intended to be either Palestine, to which many hoped to go soon, or the homes of relatives in America and elsewhere.

The youngsters arrived in groups ranging from fifty to three-hundred individuals. The first reached England in August 1945. Others followed every few months.

My memory of their arrival is still very vivid. I was among the staff who were assembled in Windermere to prepare a hostel in the barracks where the young people were to spend the first three months of their stay in England.

They had flown all day from Prague to Carlisle, accompanied by UNNRA officials, and most of them arrived very airsick. They had been held up for hours, because a fourteen-year-old stowaway had needed to be dealt with first. By the time all the formalities had been gone through, and they had been driven by bus from Carlisle to Windermere, it was late at night—the same night incidentally, when on the other side of the globe, frightened emissaries of their Emperor were asking for an armistice with General MacArthur's troops. This was the night of the fifteenth of August 1945, which ended the war.

The children stepping down from the buses seemed lively enough, and to our surprise appeared to be well fed, though wearing badly worn-out clothes. Each had a suitcase. They immediately started to talk excitedly in Yiddish and broken German, telling horror stories which they threw at us in a wild and disorderly fashion. It was as if they wanted to give us their credentials through a nightmare of horrific accounts, which rushed out as if a dam had burst. Its flow hardly stopped during the first few days. They rattled off their tales, excitedly and apparently without emotion, and we had to listen.

On that first night they were led into the main building where they had to strip off and leave their clothes and suitcases to be disinfected on the spot. These precautions were taken for fear of typhus and other infectious diseases which were then still prevalent in camps on the continent. They stood wrapped in blankets in one of the big rooms, waiting their turn to be examined by one of the doctors who had come to check them over and give them the go-ahead before they could be led to their respective barracks.

We had the impression of young men and women, fat, flabby of flesh, with very rounded limbs, both boys and girls looking much the same in this respect. The boys had developed fat breasts, big tummies and rounded feminine hips. The girls looked more like young women than young girls. We mistakenly thought some of them were pregnant because of the heaviness of their bodies.

The doctors and dentists who examined everybody thoroughly during the following weeks reported that they were less healthy than they looked, were mostly overweight and suffering vitamin deficiency. It was advised that they should not exert themselves. Their teeth were in a deplorable condition; they had poor immunity so were likely to develop infections from any scratches or small wounds, and they were suffering from minor skin conditions.

Their enormous vitality was, however, apparent at first sight, and so was their general friendliness. They appeared biddable and followed us willingly when we led them in small groups to their respective lodgings in the pitch dark. For the former inhabitants of Auschwitz Extermination Camp this whole performance must have been linked up with associations of a special kind, but none of them objected. They allowed the procedure to go through all its stages, even though it is understandable that some of them might have thought this was the moment when fate had caught up with them. A few had anxious questions as to where other groups had disappeared to and what the light in front of the barracks meant. Some had a halting and hesitant way of following the guide, but these were the only signs by which you could have guessed. There was no resistance, though afterwards, a few confessed to their misgivings.

My job this first night was to be a guide to these groups. I remember trying to give comfort by telling them hot baths were waiting for them. I knew nothing yet of the details of the preparation for the gas chambers in Auschwitz, in which a bath was offered in the same way as the last act before extermination. I realised later I must have contributed considerably to their anxieties through this remark. Luckily, the little presents, the flowers and sweets which they found in each cubicle, soon convinced them that a different kind of business was meant here, in spite of the hygiene ritual which had initiated the entry into a free country for them in the same way as it would have done into Hitler's gas chambers.

By four o'clock in the morning, the last bus had left empty and everybody had settled into the barracks. We had had many misgivings as to the type of children we would get as our charges, expecting young gangsters, and were exhilarated and astonished to find we were wrong. So, these friendly boys and girls were the former inmates of concentration camps! These children would be our charges. They had told us with urgency that they wanted to learn and to have lessons, holding up six fingers to indicate the six years of school life they had missed. These were not remotely the toughs we were prepared to meet.

There was only one occasion on the first night when we heard sounds that made us think they were starting to be rowdy. In one of the barracks, a boy was standing in front of a closed door which led into one of the cubicles and kicking it with all his might. A crowd of other boys had surrounded him and were shouting and laughing. I rushed there and offered my help asking whether anybody had been shut in by mistake.

'Nobody is inside,' said the boy who was kicking, 'but I can knock at my own door now.'

It was the realisation that he was to have a room of his own which had caused him to show his pleasure in this riotous way. The cubicles were minute, but it was the first time in six years that the boys and girls had been given privacy.

We had criticised this arrangement earlier, saying these former prisoners would feel imprisoned again in these tiny rooms. We would have preferred large friendly rooms ourselves but had not succeeded in finding that sort of accommodation for the children. Many of the boys and girls told us later that nothing was as important for them in those first days as 'a room for each'. I am reporting this, because it was an example of the unpredictability which we experienced on first contact with these youngsters, and which became even more intense over the course of the following weeks. The characteristics of the young survivors were still a mystery to us. All our guesses were wrong at first, and we had to learn about them while our astonishment grew.

In talking about the first few months of their stay and my observations of this group, I will often be guilty of giving the impression that all of them were, or did, or said something. It should, of course, be understood that for every statement I make in sweeping terms, it would be easy to find exceptions among those three hundred individuals to prove the opposite. These exceptions are of no less interest than the rule, but as long as this report deals with the first arrivals, when our contact and knowledge of them was limited to little more than general impressions, I shall have to neglect this important minority. I am less able than the other members of staff to talk about individuals in this group. The jobs I did for them were varied and I changed from one service to another in quick succession, which prevented me from having more intimate contact with any of them. Later on, when I describe the intensive training of a group of eleven girls, I will be able to give a more detailed description of each individual's opinions, attitudes and reactions as I met them in our work.

On the first night, in my own little cubicle, following the impact of my first impressions, I made the following resolution. I would not allow any personal relationship to develop between myself and the youngsters in my charge. I felt guilty in front of them and was the wrong person to be a substitute parent in their new lives. This camp would have my hands and brain, but my heart could not accept the claim which the children could make on me as orphans. I shrank back from the enormity of the task, knowing that I could not bear it.

And so, I taught them English, drawing and painting. I helped in the clothing department and in the dining room. I supervised the two barracks which had been assigned to me by our leader, but I left the real work to be done there to the young helpers almost completely. I also helped occupy the patients in the little hospital we ran.

The First Day

On the morning of the first day, we tried to find suitable clothes for those who needed them most. To our dismay, we found that the flannels, shirts, jackets, shoes and socks we had stocked for them were mostly unsuitable. We had been told we should prepare for a hundred and eighty fifteen-year-old boys, forty-eight girls of the same age, fifty thirteen-year-old boys and twenty children who would be much younger. We had ordered clothes accordingly. The older boys and girls, some two hundred and fifty out of three hundred, could not wear what we had stocked because of their abnormally sized bodies. Also, they were not fifteen years old, but nearer seventeen, with some even older. They had lied to the authorities and given a younger birth date. This had been easily done as they were much shorter than they should have been, due to six years of a starvation diet. The flesh they had put on after liberation, and which made them now look heavy, was not healthy muscle but unhealthy fat. Their bodies changed back to normal only over the course of many months.

Lying must have been a frequent occurrence in the years under Nazi rule. They had learned to lie about their names. It had proved useful (by saving them from being sent to the gas chambers) to be sometimes more than twelve years old, sometimes less. You could not predict the outcome, but it could be vitally important. A number was tattooed on the forearm, with no indication of name, age, or place of origin. They had learned to be flexible with respect to their identity, which became increasingly vague. It took quite a time for many before they were capable of revealing it to us.

In reality, there were very few small boys and girls of Jewish origin left alive in the concentration camps at the end of hostilities. They had all either been systematically exterminated together with their mothers as 'unfit for labour' or were too frail to survive the hunger and disease which in the disorganized state of collapsing Germany was responsible for the death of hundreds and thousands who otherwise would still have been found alive at the end of the war. The older ones, being hardier, had survived, having passed the selection in Auschwitz as 'fit for labour'.

In our case they had cheated the Home Office, because the permits were officially to be given only to people who had not yet reached their sixteenth birthday.

The hostel was situated at the bottom of a flat valley which widened towards Lake Windermere. It consisted of orderly rows of barracks with tidy lanes between them. The surrounding mountainsides were covered by woods, and the valley itself was partly grassland, partly gardens belonging to the occupants of the camp. These people had been employed in the aircraft factory nearby for some years but were now working a very restricted schedule which is how we had succeeded in obtaining accommodation in the 'unmarried quarters'. The 'married quarters' were still occupied by the workers' families.

On the sixteenth of August the weather was brilliant, but none of our new guests could venture out as their clothes were not yet back from the fumigation vans. Only the children of the English families were playing in the lanes as usual. By noon, the whole picture had changed. Our boys and girls started to swarm out and immediately the local population turned up, showing their curiosity about the boys and girls of whose whereabouts they had been informed. They had

*NB not sixteenth August it should read on the fifteenth August

16

expressed a willingness to bear with us at a meeting we had held to make contact and establish the necessary friendly relationship with those whom they might have considered intruders. There were, of course, grave misgivings on both sides as to how it would be to have former young concentration camp inhabitants among the ordinary British working-class population. Despite the misgivings, it worked very well indeed. Our boys and girls could hardly believe it when they learned that these friendly people were English folks and not Jews, and that they did not mind when they 'borrowed' their bicycles for a ride, and indeed, afterwards offered them the use of them spontaneously; who stopped in the lanes to teach them, laughingly, a few words of English; who invited them into their homes, and even installed a wireless set for them in the open so that a large group could listen to talks in Polish. It all made a great impression on them. 'This is a good country,' they said. 'These are good people.'

In fact, the local residents of the district, the educational authorities, the medical profession and even the weather worked together to welcome them.

Of course, we had to be prepared to see some of our charges take to the countryside and try to disappear for good. We had talked this situation through before their arrival and had agreed that we would not take action in such cases. We were pleased and astonished to find that by nightfall everybody was back, although we had not asked any of the boys or girls to follow any rules as yet.

Questions of Discipline and Order

We had undertaken many discussions in which we planned our work before the three hundred arrived. All agreed that our future charges should be relieved as much as possible of any feeling of pressure exerted by an authority, particularly by an authority made up of strangers. Once they knew us and our intentions towards them, we could start to introduce rules and regulations, but not before then. We accepted the potential for both major and minor disasters, but we understood it would be useless to try to enforce rules at first, and this could badly spoil their chances for a healthy rehabilitation in the future if we did not take this line. Everyone worked in this way from the very start.

The fact that no major disaster occurred can be ascribed to this attitude, this lack of pressure and the resulting atmosphere of ease (through chaos).

None of the boys or girls attempted suicide in these first critical weeks, none of them tried to kill anyone, and nobody injured themselves badly or became seriously ill. The amount of straightforward behaviour and the confidence which was characteristic in their conversations with us showed their trust in the sanity of their surroundings, and must have helped them, and still be helping them in no measurable degree. Mr O.F., the appointed organiser and leader of the camp has to take credit for that success.

My first attempt to introduce a rule into our chaotic community life went like this. It was the third morning of their stay among us, before breakfast, when most of the boys were lounging around in the vicinity of the barracks. With the help of the young students, we gathered most of them together on the porch in front of the building. I addressed them, saying I thought it would be a good idea if we could arrange a signal which could be heard from afar to tell everybody they were needed at the barracks for a specific reason, such as to assemble for an outing, or to plan some activity or lesson, etc. They all agreed it would be good to have such a sign. When I asked what we could use, they proposed a whistle. One of the boys produced one from his pocket. I took it and asked what kind of a signal they thought would be appropriate. They suggested three short sharp blows. When I wanted to try this out, just to be sure that everybody would recognise the call, they tore the whistle from my hands and forbade me to use it.

'No, not you, one of the men must blow it.'

It was given to one of the young student helpers who managed a sharp, shrill blow. The boys approved. I repeated the explanation: whenever it was heard, it meant they were wanted back at their hut. We talked about a few other things, but attention soon waned, and they dispersed.

After breakfast, when again almost everybody was near their hut, half an hour after our first assembly, I wanted to test this out. The young student blew the whistle. Three sharp blows rang out over the estate. Many of the forty boys who had proposed and agreed to this signal were within our sight. The others must have been within hearing distance, but not one turned his head, not one moved towards the hut. Not one turned up.

Later in the day when I asked them to explain this inconsistency, they were perfectly clear.

'You can't expect us to come because a whistle is blown. Not now.'

'Why?'

'Because when an SS guard wanted us to come, he also blew a whistle, and in the same way, but the SS men had their truncheons and rifle butts to see that we came quickly. Then we had to obey. Now we cannot. Not if there is nothing else than the blow of a whistle.'

It had been their choice, this whistle blowing, because they knew of no other way or sign. In freedom the old signal did not work. Luckily!

Later that afternoon, the UNNRA Official who had organised their transport and accompanied them left our camp. The boys and girls wanted to say goodbye, so at the appointed time, more than two hundred boys plus the girls marched military-style to the square in front of the central hall and formed a quadrangle. They were led by a young man of twenty-two years who had come under the permit system with them, and who apparently looked on himself as their leader. This young Polish Jew had played an important role inside the camps in the Jewish Zionist Underground movement.

One of the boys made an excellent farewell speech while the assembled youngsters stood to attention. Then they sang a few choruses, gave the Zionist salute, and marched off again in formation in the shortest possible time, under the command of their leader. An S.S. battalion could not have functioned more precisely. How had they achieved this? It was due to the young man who had been their leader throughout the previous months. They still acknowledged him in that capacity, but there would be no further opportunity for him to use his authority while he was with us.

There was another puzzling aspect of their behaviour which made it difficult to carry out the arrangements which we all had to agree upon. On innumerable occasions, when we were leading an eager group in a lesson or discussion, we found they did not want to stop when the dinner bell rang, and only grumblingly broke up after being assured they could continue with this apparently fascinating subject at the appointed hour in the near future. Yet on the next day, at the appointed time, nobody would turn up.

They had no worries for the future, if it's possible to say such a thing. Their memories of the past were problematic, but any future plans seemed to hold no promise or possibility of realisation, nor any obligation on their part to make their fulfilment possible. It was as if the Nazis had succeeded with these youngsters in wiping out the capacity to take the future seriously, to wish for a future, or to believe in the reality of the future eventually becoming the present. Perhaps it was because for six years of their young lives, the future had held too many possibilities which were coupled with fear, and too few, if any, to which they could look forward. This was quite apart from the fact that in a prisoner's life there is no room for planning—so the whole mechanism of successful forward planning was now out of gear. They could not remember what had been planned or make up their minds to execute that plan when the right time came by changing the future into the present.

Or perhaps it was because the one thing which had meant 'future' to them throughout those long years—the reunion with their families and the possibility of living at home again—had failed them and not materialised, so they could not now believe in the ability to make a wished-for future become a reality.

Activities and Lessons

I have already spoken of the discussions and lessons. We started them as soon as possible with lessons in English. Only two or three among them had any knowledge at all of spoken English. Most did not know a single word yet, but all of them realised it was the most important thing for them to learn.

There were very few English people among the staff. We were mostly German and Austrian refugees. The language which we used in talking to them therefore was German, because this was the only one which we had in common as they had learned much of it during their life in the concentration camps. Though hardly any of them spoke it well, they could make themselves easily understood by also using Yiddish. The Jewish background of their vocabulary may have been the reason why their way of expressing themselves reminded us often of biblical language, though this was not only through their use of words. Their way of thinking and expressing their thoughts and experiences through parallels and symbols was, I think, what produced the biblical impression even more than the vocabulary.

From the third day onwards, we gave regular English lessons to small groups sitting in the grass, on the porches, or under a tree. Their attendance was much lower than expected given that their expressions of keenness to learn had sounded so genuine. Why, then, did so disappointingly few turn up for the lessons? Were they not sincere; were they not so keen after all? One possible explanation was that our lessons were not good enough. We had no textbooks as yet, and no experience as we were not qualified teachers. It was also very hard for them to concentrate on anything for any length of time, with the exception of a few boys among them who retired to their rooms with their study books and spent much of the night studying, therefore making very good progress. Some other subjects were also introduced, mathematics being the most successful.

On the first Sunday of their stay, that is on the fourth day after their arrival, they gave us a performance. None of us had helped with the preparations. Speaking Yiddish, they enacted witty scenes in the good old Jewish traditions, presenting typical scenes from Jewish-Polish village life. The performance was humorous, very humane, well-acted, full of self-criticism of an endearing, mellow kind, and gave us real pleasure. One of the boys played two fugues by Bach on the piano. This was not showing off. He was not ham-fisted. He went on to study at the Royal Academy of Music in London.

The hall in Windermere was packed to capacity. Some of the local residents of the estate were there as well. It must have made an exceedingly strange impression on them, but they seemed to enjoy the happy atmosphere, which I am sure nobody who was within those four walls with us could avoid.

A large part of the show comprised choral singing. The singing of psalms and other religious songs is very much practised in Orthodox Jewish homes, and these Jewish melodies are very beautiful. They have a style of their own. The young voices of the children, among whom there were a few very good ones, rang out into the English summer evening, Eastern, sweet, heavy, and very poignant in their rhythm. The songs went on through many verses, the repetition of which gave the new listeners the impression they had heard something old and familiar, rather than something new.

I remember how this choral singing stirred me more than anything else had done. It made me cry. We were all over-tired by then. We had not had enough sleep, due to the non-stop bathing which went on in the huts. There was hardly any break between the last shower-bath of the night, and the first one in the small hours of the morning. According to the children, there was no time which was not the right time for a bath.

At first, we had thought they had been overwhelmed by the unaccustomed luxury of the very normal shower installations, and this was the explanation for their excessive displays of cleanliness. But on investigation, we discovered that they had had the use of shower-baths in many of the camps, and that to be clean was one of the precautions they had to take, because to be found dirty, or with a spot on the skin, meant extermination. They did not have this to fear in Windermere, and they knew it, but they still were preoccupied with an anxiety that they were not clean enough and they were therefore over-zealous with their personal cleanliness. The hours they chose to wash their underwear and shirts were equally irregular and frequent.

When we asked them to do the necessary cleaning of their barracks, however, it was very difficult to get teams together for this purpose, just as it was difficult to get them to help in the dining room. This was because, as I noted earlier, you could not count on any arrangement which was made with them, particularly if it was supposed to be regularly repeated. They could not be relied on at all at this stage, but rather the reverse was true.

The Clothing Problem

The clothing question overshadowed the first few weeks in Windermere. As mentioned previously, the abnormality of their figures meant there were not enough well-fitting garments for them in the stores when they arrived, and they had to be patient before they could all receive the promised, and often necessary, new outfit. Only those who were there with us could understand what a problem this was during this period. It became a preoccupation for everyone, not only the boys and girls, to solve the clothing problem as quickly as possible.

As well as this lack of appropriate clothing, which was accentuated by rationing difficulties and scarcity of material, there was something else which aggravated the situation to a severe degree. The urgency of the requests the children made, the impatience which resulted from the delay, the twists and turns which their minds, unaccustomed to fulfilment took, even when their claims were reasonably well met, made them refuse good, well-fitting clothes when they were offered. This must all have had a deeper cause than sheer impatience. What was it that justified in their eyes the fantastic importance which they attached to this getting of new clothes?

In my opinion, it had become a way for the young boys and girls to focus on and concentrate the grudges they had held as victims. It was the first occasion on which they were being given something personally, by one of us—in other words, by a person, and not an institution. It therefore gave them a chance to show jealousy, distrust and despair at their own value, and all the range of difficult human emotions from which they suffered, and which for the first time had a chance to be expressed. Their rooms, their meals, the outings, the little presents and sweets were the same for all, but in the provision of clothing there was variety, difference in quality, and the possibility of choice. In the clothing store, each child was served individually by one of us. Even the infinite patience which people exercised there could not work miracles. It was no wonder that the superintendent of the clothing stores was the first to have a nervous breakdown. She was made to feel personally responsible by the boys for the difficulties they encountered. Her task was the most difficult of all.

During the weeks in which the boys had to wait for their newly ordered suits to be delivered, they knew that there were still clothes in the stores. They had tried them on over and over again, but they still crowded in front of the closed entrance, hammering against it, trying to force an entry, sometimes successfully breaking in. They tried in vain to find something which would fit them or which they would like to wear. This last point was perhaps the most important to them. If you watched them making their choice, you often got the impression that, violently keen as they were in their desire to find something, there was still a discontent in them, a demonstrable disgust, which at the last moment stopped many of them accepting a good and well-fitting garment. After much coaxing they might be persuaded once in a while to accept it and take it to their room, only to return it the next day, sometimes literally flinging it in our faces and turning it down as an impossibility and a disgrace.

We had all seen big boys of sixteen and seventeen, who in many ways were older and more experienced than their age, behave in the clothes store like unreasonable four-year-olds, flying into a rage or bursting into tears because what they wanted was not to be had. If you take that literally, I think you come near enough to an explanation of their behaviour. It was not because the sleeves of a pullover were short, or the pattern of a shirt was 'wrong' that it was deemed unacceptable. Their refusal to be contented by any of us at that stage was due to the great depth of the fact that 'what they wanted was not to be had'.

Some facts relating to their past

When the first week was over, we were still being surprised as our knowledge of them increased. It was like the gradual reveal of a panorama. The figures of these young people emerged, distinctive in their directness, against a background of cruelty and suffering unheard of in our becalmed Western world. They seemed to move without either searching for a path or scrutinising the scenery through which they went, but looking backwards, with a strained expression. Always alone, though never single, they revealed by their behaviour—a generosity and readiness to give and take—an awareness that there were other people on this earth. They lived among us, oblivious of time, compact of will, with the experience of hell ever-present in their minds and an intensity which our life of compromise did not permit us. They hoped for a better future without quite believing in it yet, but with the knowledge in their hearts that they had fooled Hitler, and that life was there to be lived.

The telling of horror stories had decreased by the second week, though an orderly historical presentation of their experiences was a feat most of would not be ready for until much later. When they felt able to produce written reports, it gave us a clearer concept through the sequence of facts and experiences of what it meant to be a Polish Jewish child in the year 1945 or, in other words, to have survived six years of persecution.

At that stage, four months after liberation, what they were telling us had already taken on a romantic character for them, in my opinion. They obviously had met reporters on the continent and had experienced the feeling of importance that resulted from the impression their stories made on the listener. Their experiences were unique. They evoked pity, and their telling had proved profitable. They could ameliorate their situation by telling their stories. All this was reason enough to go on telling them to new acquaintances—which we were. But at that stage, if they told their stories to each other, it was with a great display of excitement, whereas when talking to us, they seemed detached and unemotional.

I remember how, on the third day in the afternoon, when I had retired to my cubicle for an hour's rest, I heard the most detailed and horrifying description of camp and transport scenes going on next door. I thought one of my colleagues must be there with a few of the boys who were telling him or her their stories. After a little while, when I was becoming too disturbed, I got up and went into their room to ask them to kindly move to another cubicle for a while because I needed to rest. When I opened the door, I found there were only boys in the room, crowded onto the bed and floor, telling each other their stories—and not one of us among them.

They had been reciting what I labelled these horror stories, which were not their most personal experiences, and nothing to do with the loss of their homes and their closest family. They were the stories of the hunger transport which had happened during the last weeks of Nazi Regime, in a situation of chaos, when they were moved about on unscheduled trains, by the most roundabout routes, or on foot, pushed along by the rifle butts of the SS guards, from the concentration camps in the West, which were threatened to be overrun by the American and British armies, to the East, where the Nazis hoped to hold out longer against the Russians who were fast advancing in the opposite direction. These journeys had lasted from three to five weeks, with no provision for food or water along the way. Only a very small percentage of people survived, the last links in the chain which crowned their feats of endurance.

These events were the foremost subjects of their tales at this time. The deprivations which they had suffered during this transportation were described by many of them with the same tone of pride and subtle boasting with which we told each other our bomb stories. This experience had been shared by most of them. Almost everybody who came with this first consignment to us had taken part in this hunger transport, the terminus of which was Theresienstadt.

Theresienstadt, also called Terezin, is a small town on the Czechoslovak border, not far from the German border. At the beginning of the war the Nazis had evacuated its normal population and turned it into a ghetto, housing Jewish prisoners from Austria, Germany, and Czechoslovakia. Many of the Jews from Vienna, Berlin and Prague had spent weeks, months or years in the ghetto of Theresienstadt before being sent to extermination camps in Poland. The overcrowding in the ghetto, which was very bad throughout its existence, became extreme in the last few weeks of the war, when the survivors of the transports which arrived from all the concentration camps all over Germany were added to its numbers.

The descriptions of the adult inhabitants of the ghetto of Theresienstadt at that time, who had helped in giving first aid to these starved children, tallied exactly with the tales of the boys and girls. It was mostly dead bodies that were extracted from the cattle vans which were used for these transports, but in each of them there were a few, who, though resembling skeletons, were still alive.

In the anonymously written book, The Dark Side of the Moon (Faber & Faber, 1946), there are accurate descriptions of similar transports. Though the victims in those vans were Polish prisoners, evacuated by the Russians to the Siberian provinces, the conditions under which hundreds of thousands travelled, survived, and died, and the experiences and reactions of the inmates of these cattle vans, were identical to what we know of the transports in Germany for which the Nazis were responsible. For details, therefore, I am referring to this publication.

Among this first batch of stories there were also some which had nothing to do with the transport but were set in the concentration camps. One, which I heard from different boys, all of whom said that they had seen it, was the story of a small child being torn in two. It may have happened. It may have happened repeatedly or never. It may have happened in front of some of our young people. Whether it was fantasy or reality, we do not know. The first time I heard it was when I looked at the ring on one of the boys' fingers, a death's head ring, the sign of a dignitary of the SS, which the boy had taken from one of the guards when they were set free.

Our impression was that these tales, which described the excesses of mankind in orgies of sadism, probably contained a mixture of both truth and fantasy, which the one who told the story was as little aware of, and just as muddled by, as the listener.

I knew that in my effort to do my duty by the children, and to be the right receptacle for what they needed to throw away, I could not allow myself to be swept away by pity, as that would not be the best way of forming relationships for these boys and girls. For them, it mattered that friendship had roots other than pity, and therefore I had to listen and appear as unmoved as possible. This was extremely difficult, and I remember being exhausted by it. Twice, I had to save myself from breaking down in front of them by pretending I had no time to listen. I had to stop myself understanding that what these young tongues were telling me had actually happened to the young people who stood in front of me. In order to bear it more easily, I pretended to be listening to a new version of Grimm's Fairy tales.

For as long as we were new acquaintances, we were told these stories. Later on, when we got to know each other better, they started to tell us about their personal tragedies. It was easier to listen then.

The impression I gathered was that it was not so much that they had had to witness these horrors— living under such deprivations and cruelty had not done them irreparable damage—it was more the losses they had suffered; the way they had lost their families. Such circumstances, at much too early an age, had left them desperate, insecure, with a feeling of guilt which they were all suffering: guilt at being alive. I have heard many accounts which prove this, some simple direct statements, some veiled, but all unmistakably saying the same thing.

They had shared their Odysseys with hundreds of thousands of other young people. Broadly speaking, it had been the same for all. But they had survived, while the others had been killed. Typically, they would ask if there was anything that could account for their survival. Was it their physical strength? Had it been by pure chance? Were they conditioned for it by their family background? Was it to do with the personality of the survivor?

It would be fascinating to discover the difference in the survivors and be able to delineate any specific personality traits.

This problem presented itself to us very soon, though not in the form of questions. Yes, these are the ones who survived, was our experience, and we expressed it in these same words very soon after their arrival. Their obvious strength, their simplicity and sanity and wit were so impressive and convincing it was very easy to credit them with all the qualities necessary to affect survival. I was able to discern some of the more subtle features of this personality in my later and more intimate contact with the few whom I had the privilege to teach. Only then did I detect their innate sense for the fundamental; the integrity with which they approached their own problems; the extent to which they were capable of grasping a situation's psychological implications; and, above all, the length to which their endurance could be stretched without weakening their resolve to bear their lives. I think that during the first months of their stay in Windermere, this resolve was very much tested.

In the camps and ghettoes, they had lived under an enormous strain, but everybody else had lived under the same strain. Fate, with a capital F, had ruled supreme. The suffering was common. It had been shared by everybody. The world outside the camp and the life there had no meaning. They had all lived in order to be alive on the day of liberation. Life, hard as it was, had an aim. When the doors of the prison opened, they would find their families again, and live with them again, but for the young people we had here, this hope had not been fulfilled. Only a handful of them had a near relative still living.

After recovering from typhus, which they had caught either on the transport or immediately afterwards in Theresienstadt, they had, in the four months between liberation and coming to England, travelled thousands of miles. They had crisscrossed Europe in search of their relations. By rail, jeep and lorry, recognisable by their shorn hair, helped by allied soldiers and by the civilian population of many countries, they had followed rumours and crossed borders to and fro, trying to track down the people who were nearest to them, and who, in the end, they failed to find.

They had carried provisions and clothes to Poland by the permission of the Russian Commander, who, at his entry into Theresienstadt, had thrown open the vast storehouses of the ghetto. There, they had bartered these goods, or left them behind. When they had spent all their resources, without results, they came back to Theresienstadt for more, in order to go on with their search. Many had been in Belgium or France, had gone from camp to camp in Germany, because somebody somewhere said they had seen or heard of a person of such and such a name here or there. Only after they had given up their search as hopeless, having returned to Theresienstadt, their 'last address' so to speak, and after they had made up their minds that they would like to go to Palestine, and that to go via England would be quicker than waiting on the Continent, was the mechanism in place to bring them here. But on the peaceful shores of Lake Windermere, after the first exaltation of having arrived had vanished, it felt to them as if they had fallen into a vacuum.

I quote directly from my notes of that time:

August 18th (that is the fourth day after their arrival)

Walked for a while behind B.C. and L.G. listened to their talk in Yiddish. B.C. obviously very worried: 'One is not a stone, thrown into this world. One is a human being, properly born. One has parents and brothers and sisters. Even if one has nothing learned, like us, one has thoughts in one's head. One can't help it. I have one thought in my head. It turns round and round. It is, "What for?"'

Find D.H. standing with a forlorn expression on his face on the path between the huts. He does not move on but stares ahead of him as if he had, in the middle of a walk, forgotten to go on. Asked him whether he was feeling alright. D.H. 'No, not good.' Then, shrugging his shoulders, he says, 'I am homesick for the streets and the people as they are at home. How can I be well? My parents, my four sisters—I had four sisters, beautiful sisters—you know what I mean—everybody dead.'

I asked him when he had been separated from them.

D.H. had a ticket, a ticket from the labour office. 'When the SS came, they asked who had a

ticket. All those who had a ticket had to go to the left. I went to the left. Then to all the others…'
Here he stopped with tears in his eyes and said, 'You understand. I would have preferred to go
with the rest of my family. We would have been all together.'

I asked him whether he had any relatives still alive. He said, 'No I am all alone by myself. I do
not know what to do.' I suggested he go and see Mr. F. with whom the boys were starting to have
a very good relationship, but he declined. 'No I don't want to do anything at all.'

All the barracks reported that the mood was deteriorating, and a depression had set in.

Painting in Windermere

By the end of the first week, arrangements had been made so that whoever wanted to draw or
paint could do so every afternoon in one of the larger rooms in the main building. We used the
following method. A wide choice of materials was spread out on a table in an attractive fashion,
like a buffet, near the entrance to the room. The boys and girls who came in were given to
understand that they could choose freely, use as much or as little, and stay as long or as short a
time as they liked. They received no suggestions as to what to create from me, nor any criticism,
ever. The only comment I would make was of approval. They would hear me say, 'Thank you,
lovely,' to everything they produced, irrespective of whether it was good, very poor, unfinished,
beautiful, a smudge, appealing or appalling. This approach could never claim to be a method of
teaching painting, but it was obvious that children who had suffered emotionally would profit
from using a medium specifically suited to the expression and release of emotional tension.

When we had provided the facilities to draw and paint as described, sixteen children came into
the art room on the first day and created pictures. They took to it easily and asked no questions.
It was very quiet in there, with only a few words exchanged in whispers. I was asked afterwards,
by people who had looked in, how I had achieved that. They described it as feeling like being
in church. This was true. The boys and girls behaved very differently making art to how they
behaved on other occasions. They were always extremely talkative and noisy when in groups
together, outside the art sessions. In the English lessons—where I had had a chance to make the
comparison, because I had given some English lessons myself—they talked to each other at the
top of their voices freely while the lessons were in progress. When we went out for walks, they
sang if they were not talking. In the dining room, they banged plates and cutlery, scraped chairs
across the floor, talked loudly, and even shouted. Yet in the art room they behaved 'as in church'.
It was easy to see they were deeply absorbed in the activity.

For many years, these boys and girls had no materials they could use freely. I cannot think of any
country or community in which this level of poverty is suffered so much by growing children. Even
in the worst city slums children can find cane, boards, rags and bricks to play with, quite apart
from the pencils and paper which they have at school. The material the children of the camps
had met so far had been in munition factories, in the quarries, on the roads and on building sites,
waiting to be handled by them endlessly as bags, logs and stones, carried until they were at the
point of exhaustion, exasperating their patience and breaking into their emergency reserves of
physical and nervous strength. Work in kitchens and factories held more possibilities, but even

here the monotony, the ten, twelve, or fourteen-hour days, the pace at which the work had to be done and the atmosphere of compulsion, removed any real opportunity for handling material freely. Those who had been put to do work in engineering plants and garages had suffered least from this deprivation. For most of them, though, this was the first chance they had had to be creative. Here was material—plentiful, good material—to be used by them as they liked. I have never seen a group fall so completely and deeply under the spell of a material which gives of itself; which can be made to tell the things about which one cannot speak.

I was very much keyed up for their painting. I had worked in the same way with groups of children in London shelters after the Blitz and had seen their enthusiasm. I had seen what they had painted, I had seen the changes in their work, followed the ups and downs in their moods led by what they had expressed in their paintings. I knew nothing about them, other than what I learnt through their work: nothing of their past, nothing of their present life, other than the shelter that had become their home because London was being bombed. But they had given me a chance to see something of their inner life through their paintings. In this way, I had learnt about their fears and growing confidence, their wishes and urges, the balance they had achieved or their struggle for it. I felt this had showed me their truth. I did not have sufficient knowledge to interpret precisely what I was seeing, yet I knew the children understood their unspoken confidences had been accepted by me and were welcomed.

In Windermere the situation looked similar enough, so I did not think I would get into difficulties. I had called the painting with the shelter children an experiment. I had felt aloof and I was not interested in the individual. All I was keenly interested in was the question of, 'What will they paint tonight?' I had wanted to compare and to count, and I enjoyed the variations and the repetitions. I had tried to get a glimpse of the loss, and of the paths which creative action follows.

At Windermere, I expected it would be the same, but I quickly found it was not. I could not help but relate the pictures which were made to the youngster who was making them, so this became a means of knowing more of them individually. I had shied away from having a personal relationship with the camp children, but now I had produced in the art room an opportunity for them to talk to me most intimately about their most private life. I had slipped in by the back door after I had barred myself from the front. Yes, I could use the material for statistics as much as I liked. I could admire the simplicity and the strength of their expression, but there was no getting away from it.

More than anything else, it was a picture made by Chaim, Aaron and Judith, whom I knew had experienced camp life, which stayed with me. And it was Aaron, Chaim and Judith, who now tried to describe how and what they had experienced. I was forced to know more about it, forced to have a personal interest. I had managed to blur the sharpness of impression when they had said, 'We have seen this, we have lived like that.' The 'we' suited my purpose. It made evasive action possible for me.

The pictures I now saw laboriously produced spoke of the desolation wrought in each individual child. Many were big and bold—a gravestone filling half a sheet of wrapping paper; a stretch of barbed wire tearing through a white sheet, with one guard in the middle; a plain of grass cut into shreds by black lines—documents which evaporated a screaming emptiness. These were more painful than their tales, and, in their rigidity, gave away the secret of the silent effort which must have enabled survival.

The children made very limited use of the possibilities of colour mixing. They kept to hard and simple ranges of primaries, using red or blue as if the red and blue on their dish were the only red and blue in the world. They seemed completely detached from any attempt at naturalistic colouring. It often happened that they would choose an utterly unrealistic colour, such as when they painted trees with red, brown and black predominant. I looked in vain for the playfully inaccurate running of paint which invites fantasy and lures the artist to new and bolder adventures.

Another striking feature in some of their work was an inclination to leave a gap in the middle of the picture between the earth and the sky, in the way eight and nine-year-old children who start making landscapes work often enough. Many of these seventeen-year-old boys and girls did the same thing. Sometimes the gap was very wide, sometimes even accentuated by an outline. It prevented the sky from touching the earth.

Some of them had an odd way of painting a picture first, and then making a negative version of the same thing, without realising they had done so.

Here is an example:

A pattern on a blue background with diagonal branches in white, and green leaves with a spot of red in them, repeated and changed by the same boy on the same evening into a white background with blue branches. The leaves stayed green as they were, but changed direction, the red spots left them and consolidated into one big square of block of red which bore Hitler's aggressive insignia. There was a well-known German proverb written underneath, which translated would be: work is the sweetness of life.

The boy who drew the picture brought it to me. He explained with a sneer on his face that this was the inscription which was put in large letters at the entrance of the camp, for everybody who entered it to read. The cynicism of the quote had been paired by him with the 'negative' in his symbolical pictorial production. I am sure he was unaware he had done this. His pictures had as little conscious meaning to him as any of the children's.

Here is some statistical data for comparison with the material from the shelters.

Sixty-six boys and girls painted over the course of two weeks, after which the art room was closed down. There were a hundred and fifty-five attendances in all. The difference in execution was striking. The shelter children smudged and splashed about with paint. The work of the children from the camps was painfully accurate and neat, with a severe and oppressive restraint in evidence. Another striking difference was the number of attempts the camp children had made to describe experiences they had really lived through, in comparison with the shelter groups. Out of some two thousand five hundred pictures done by three-hundred and fifty shelter children from different London districts, there were only four which represented shelter life, and six which showed burning or bombing—experiences which all these London shelter children must have had. But the Blitz had not shaken the fundamental structures of their lives. Their families had not been broken up. They were in the shelters with their mothers and brothers and sisters. 'London burning' had been to almost all of them an experience which had not gone that deep. It did not prevent them from expressing their emotional life in the normal way through symbols used at their respective ages. They had painted, if they were boys, the innumerable boats and aeroplanes which we know so well. Girls painted mainly trees and patterns, and houses and people in large numbers, which in my experience were favourites with both sexes. In their work they had permitted themselves to speak through normal images of their fear and insecurity, of their joy and hope.

The camp children, as I have said, not only took the theme of their paintings much more often from their painful memories, but their use of symbols was unusual as well. Many, for example, painted the Star of David as their first picture. There were twenty-five pictures of the star, done by fifteen boys aged from ten to seventeen, and two girls, both nine years old, who used it on cards sent with their best wishes and love for a birthday. The Star of David was always executed with the greatest care and with the help of a ruler. Often, though, it was left unfinished, or smudged at the very last moment. It was clearly important as a symbol of their Jewish faith and origin, something they seemed very aware of. Many came from Orthodox homes. They had been made to wear the Star, by Hitler's orders, as a degrading distinction. On their drawings it appeared either alone on a sheet, or as a decoration for a house, a boat or a flag. The Jewish seven-armed candlestick was painted fifteen times.

There were hardly any pictures with people in them, and very few with aeroplanes or boats, though a few of those were done by the two little girls who also drew the Star of David. The overwhelming majority of the pictures showed houses, large or small, often surrounded by fences. Some were weirdly beautiful. Most of the houses were painted red, though the houses in Poland are not red but white-washed or distempered. The houses in the pictures stood on hillsides, or had a diagonal line as a base, making them look awkward and badly placed. Many were tiny. And the well-known friendly house, with a tree to the right and the left, was usually missing, with only three pictures in this format. In one, the tree was half-hidden behind that ever-recurring fence; on the other, one of the trees was green, the other had bare branches and appeared to be dead. In the third picture, two black ravens perched on the tree and were the main feature. The house in the distance looked empty.

There were a few pictures of animals, a few landscapes with houses included, and a few trees boldly standing alone. There were seven pictures of burning houses or towns, ten pictures of ghettos and concentration camps. A colourful painting of the Ghetto in Lwów and a pencil drawing of a concentration camp were done the by the same seventeen-year-old boy on two successive occasions. Though the ghetto picture showed the guard at the entrance and the graveyard at the back, it was still a joyful picture, full of colour and detail, and its spires and cupolas made the ghetto look like a town from a fairy tale.

The endless net of barbed wire in the picture of the concentration camp, with poles sticking out aggressively, no background, and no colour except the tiny marks of red at the door, expressed no joy of form, and made a striking contrast of mood which left me puzzled at the difference in representation of two localities, which so far we had thought had stood for pretty much the same thing. The explanation for this difference became clear when I learnt that while they lived in the ghetto the boys and girls were still together with their families. The conditions might have been overcrowded, with high levels of insecurity making it unbearable for grown-ups, but the children were still living in an unbroken family circle among parents and brothers and sisters. On the day they were sent out of the ghetto and put into concentration camps, they were alone, they had lost their families, and all security had gone. The real suffering for them started only then.

It is easy to understand how the ghetto at Lwów would have appeared to Joseph to be a paradise, full of beloved memories, which he tried to describe in bright colours even if the shadow of the graveyard is in the background. In the concentration camp picture, every single line and detail expressed the feeling of imprisonment and fear.

The art room was crowded every afternoon. I was happy to find willing assistance in the young man who I mentioned earlier in connection with the farewell ceremony for the UNNRA official, but as in the case of his first demonstration of power over the whole group, he had no further chance to exercise it. He spent the rest of his time at Windermere hanging around unhappily. He joined in with no lessons or activities, and appeared to resent the situation, but seemed very pleased with the suggestion of becoming my assistant and showed an astonishingly quick understanding of what I required regarding non-interference with the artwork. Neither he nor I did anything other than look after the materials while the sessions lasted. He was desperately anxious to be helpful, and soon he, too, started to paint. From what he told me when we cleaned the room afterwards, or filed the pictures away, I gathered he had held a responsible position within the Zionist organisation inside the concentration camps and had been a very active and aggressive young Zionist, keenly interested in politics. He needed strict order and discipline in his environment to feel comfortable, and he distrusted the free and easy-going way of life which the boys and girls led in Windermere.

I wondered how much the others were aware of his attitude, and whether this was the reason for the growing resentment of his presence in the art room. He was only a mute companion of mine, occupied with subordinate activity, yet he was a reminder of the kind of authority they had had to endure, and though they had in the beginning gladly acknowledged his role as their leader, he had now become an obstacle to their readjustment. The boys and girls avoided entering the art room if he was there and left when he entered. I could see he loved his job very much, and I had not the heart to suggest a change, but the activity in the art room declined quickly and after two weeks it had to be closed.

It is possible that I, always ready in Windermere to find fault with my own work in the handling of an individual, put too much importance on his presence as a reason for this quick decline in the use of the art room. I certainly felt guilty that I had endangered an activity which seemed profitable for many, through helping this one boy, but it is also possible that something quite different was stopping the painters from going on with their work. The sequence of their pictures often shows the last one of a series clearly linked to their sad experiences of the past. Perhaps they were frightened of being led further backwards, deeper into their misery, and they avoided this by stopping painting all together.

Mothers

This young man was not the only one among the older children who had shared the concentration camp life to some degree, and who had come to Windermere from Theresienstadt. There were a dozen other men and women who had accompanied the three hundred youngsters as escorts. Among them were three young women of whom the boys and girls said: 'They are our mothers'.

When the transport of starving prisoners from West Germany had arrived from Theresienstadt, these women had taken charge of fifty to a hundred boys and girls, all of them close to death with starvation, sick with typhus, and in a state of complete helplessness and exhaustion. They had nursed them back to life and had looked after them, helped by the ghetto authorities. They had done more for them, then and there, than the rest of us could ever do. When the boys spoke of these three women, they described what they had done for them and how they had given them their first food.

One of the women died a few weeks after her arrival in England from side-effects following surgery. She had lost her husband in the camp and her baby had been killed at birth by the Gestapo. On the day she died the camp was restless. The boys and girls hurried from one hut to another or stood around in groups. All planned activity had to stop. It was as if the community had fallen apart, and the three hundred youngsters had fallen out of the framework we had tried to construct for them. We were made very aware of the gulf between us and them. It was not only that each of them had intimately known or loved the dead woman, but also that they had lost a 'mother' again. Disaster had struck them once more.

'That one could die now!' was repeated in a crescendo with the memories of loss.

I remember being struck by the depth of compassion they showed for the cousin of the dead woman, another of the three mothers. To lose the last relative one had, meant for all of them more than just the death of a cousin.

The Little Ones

Among the three hundred children at Windermere, there were eighteen under seven years of age. The youngest among these were perhaps only three or four years old, but we had to guess their ages because their birth and origin were unknown. A few had been born in Theresienstadt. Most had been picked up when found in a desolate condition. We had no idea how they had escaped being killed by the Nazis, as all small children had been exterminated systematically, either with their mothers or immediately after birth if they were born in a ghetto. A few of the eighteen had not yet learnt to talk when they were picked up, so nobody knew their names. They therefore had had to be renamed, and this had been done in Czechoslovakia. Once in Windermere, they were settled into one of the huts which had been arranged and equipped as a nursery.

This little community of the youngest children was a very difficult environment. They were the only ones at Windermere who behaved the way we had expected all the children to behave—like frightened little animals, screaming, pulling the place to pieces, tearing toys out of each other's hands, and trying the staff severely.

I cannot give a comprehensive report on the behaviour of the youngest children as I saw very little of them, but for a month my room was in the same building as the nursery. In the early hours of every morning, I heard heart-breaking cries from there, lasting for hours. During the day I only passed them by, but often one of these poor little creatures would run towards me or after me, wanting to go with anybody, clinging, desperate to be picked up and cuddled by any stranger, all the time. The short glimpses I had of them at their play, their meals, or their walks and bath times, left me with the impression that nothing was right and normal, everything was disintegrating and was either wild and frantic, or worse, characterised by a kind of single-minded withdrawal of each child, an apathetic lack of contact with the environment. It is hard to cover the abnormality of these children in a few words, but the light of one incident might serve to demonstrate the shadow they lived within.

A nurse entered one of the nursery rooms one morning and found one of the little beds empty.

'Where is Annie?' she asked the other little occupants of the room.

'Don't know, most probably dead,' replied a four-year-old.

The little girl had only gone to the bathroom.

At this age, a normal child is at a height of emotional equilibrium, saturated with 'mother's milk' and ready to lose its first teeth. It has developed under the protection and after the image of its parents and has learnt that it is loved, that it loves and that the world around it is there to be lived in as its parents live in it. These camp babies had learnt nothing of this but had spent the past years in an emotional vacuum.

What they knew was of no use in a normal world. The Nazis had given clear proof of the old equation: absence=death. The four-year-old had learnt this lesson but knew nothing of the other equation: to exist=to be loved. She was not beloved, only looked after, and she could not love, only demand. She behaved like a wild animal because there was no orientation in her actions, no focus for her affections, no centre of gravity in her world.

The Kids

The next group in age was even smaller in numbers, comprising only eight children aged between nine and twelve. It was a mixed group of four boys and four girls, including two brothers and a sister. These were the children of a German Army General and a Jewish woman. The mother had been found one day by the Gestapo in Berlin on the street without the compulsory yellow star, so she and the children had been sent to Theresienstadt. The father who, at the time was at the Russian front, heard about it, took Army leave, and went from pillar to post to get his family back, but all in vain. The mother was sent to the gas chambers and the children stayed through the rest of the war in Theresienstadt.

Two elder sisters were among the older girls. The three younger children were the nucleus of the group of 'The Kids', and it was hard not to be upset by their ingenuity in causing trouble, disorder and alarm. They succeeded in wearing out the most-willing-to-be-amused among our younger women workers. When the woman in charge of this group went on a much-needed holiday,

I took the group over for a fortnight, and so got to know each of them a little better.

They had tremendous fights with each other, during which window panes, doors and people were hit with stones. They had things in their cupboards—other people's things—as well as frogs, dead or alive; and cats, also dead or alive. Once, a huge red signal oil lamp was taken from the borough's street repairs, only to be found lit and smoking in a locked-up cupboard in one of their cubicles. They shut each other in constantly and lost the keys. One day, when the rain had turned the lanes outside into a quagmire, and huge deep puddles had formed at the entrances to the huts, they tried to flood the huts from inside, using the firehoses and pumps.

They were invited by the milk-lorry driver to go with him on his rounds. It would have been a great relief to the community if they had stuck to his schedule, but halfway through they always got bored, left him at the most distant point, and had to be searched for, found, and fetched back. When the kindly man was asked not to take them along anymore, they cadged lifts from other vehicles, or stowed away in his lorry. Eventually we gave up looking for them. They always turned up in the evening.

On one of these evenings in October, they decided it would be nice to live on the roof of their hut. Once they had made up their minds to do something, they went ahead with it and it was no use reasoning with them. They climbed the drainpipe, took their bedding up and made themselves comfortable on the thin sooty roof, which had no railings to prevent them falling off, asleep or awake. One of our staff coaxed them down to listen to an interesting story she had to tell them. Soon the whole little group was sitting crowded around her on the grass by the side of the hut in the twilight, but the rascals refused to go inside with her. She had invited them to do so, and they listened intently, but when the story was over, one of them said, 'Is that all?' and turned round, calling, 'Come along, boys'. The little group climbed back on the roof.

When our leader arrived at the estate later on, he climbed onto the roof with the help of a ladder and made himself comfortable there among them. When night had fallen, he was still there, a big silhouette among the dwarfs on the roof, standing out amusingly against the moon and stars. When it became chilly, he finally succeeded in coaxing them down and into the hut for some chocolate and biscuits.

The two Jewish children in this group were a brother and sister. A third one, another little sister, was among the babies in the nursery. They were Hungarian, the children of a Jewish village teacher. When their parents were taken away, the father had given the boy one volume of the Talmud and told him to look after his two younger sisters and to become a rabbi. Solomon was eight years old at the time. He kept this Talmud, learning every word of it by heart so that he knew it from beginning to end and the other way around. He still had it in his possession when he came to us and knew nothing else. He was most impressive, wandering round by himself over the estate only to appear in the empty dining room in a completely absent minded fashion, murmuring sentences out of the Talmud as he meandered among the long narrow dining room tables. This child never played like other children, and he developed eating difficulties while he was with us. He slept with a candle in his cubicle because of the death of his parents and tried hard to wake up at six o'clock in the morning to go to prayers. He looked after his two younger sisters in his own way.

The elder one, Sarah, was the most determined young woman of six I ever met. She, in her turn, was just as attached to him as to the little one. Sarah had shorn hair because of ringworm and wore a red knitted hood with strings tied under her chin day and night. She had the biggest, most beautiful black eyes, in a beautiful pale face, though she had no front teeth at that time as her milk teeth had gone. Nothing could look more like a muddle between Little Red Riding Hood—because of her size and her head—and Grandma, because of her toothless mouth, her wise expression and mature features— and the wolf who had swallowed Grandma, because of her great big hungry eyes. Her personality was as rich as her looks. She treated her little sister with a mixture of intense tenderness and severity, was cautious and watchful in her contacts with grown ups, and coquettish, with a sharp wit and great independence in her behaviour towards her playmates.

The younger one among the little brothers mentioned earlier, a boy called Johann, was both her special friend and enemy. There was not an evening that the two of did not have a tussle. Johann used to watch for the moment Sarah went for her bath. Then he would race to the adjoining bathroom which was separated from Sarah by a screen seven feet high, dip his clothes in the bath and throw them, soaking wet, over the screen into Sarah's bathroom. She would start to scream, whereupon Johann would reply with shrieks of pleasure, along with his wet towel and shoes, all of which Sarah would throw back the same way.

I remember how, one evening, Johann had prepared for this joyful battle not only by collecting other people's towels, his latest venture, but also by taking a second chair into the bathroom. He balanced this second chair on the first, which was on the edge of the bathtub, then climbed onto it and clung to the screen, having first filled his mouth with soapy water from his bath. He blew this with tremendous noise and gusto onto Sarah, who was just about to step into the water. Johann dived back to refill his mouth, but Sarah had not been idle, and hit his nose with one of her shoes when he reappeared over the screen. He dropped back screaming, and a selection of swear words poured forth, uttered in sincere rage and pain, mixed in with splutterings and chokings, flavoured by nationalistic adjectives: 'Polnische Sau, ungarisches Schwein, jüdische Wanze, tschechischer Dreck, italienischer Bastard!'

When he stopped for a moment to take a breath, Sarah's voice came clear and calm over the screen wall: 'And you did not call me English?'

These three, Solomon and his two little sisters, went to a rabbi's family, where they settled very well.

Another one of the eight was Irene, the daughter of a Viennese chimney sweep and a Jewish snake dancer from Vienna's most famous entertainment park. This child, elfin in appearance and shy, had a great gift for decorating both herself and her room. Tinsels, ribbons, embroidery, little mirrors and pieces of material turned her drab cubicle into a gay place which reminded us all of a tent at a fair. Three years earlier, Irene had left Vienna and her old home when she was only six years old, but she had recreated its style at Windermere. Being of mixed origin, she became one of the charges of the Society of Friends.

Questions of creed, race and politics

The weeks passed by. Routines developed in many ways. The boys and girls took lessons in the mornings. About fifty of them started the day with prayers. An English Rabbi was among the staff, and he was in charge of the religious teaching and the Jewish ritual in the life of the camp, which we had all agreed to follow. Those of us who would not normally have done this agreed that we should all obey the laws for food and general behaviour so as not to offend the sincere beliefs of the Orthodox part of the community.

When the memory of these three months at Windermere returns, the feeling which then was so strong of living among strangers who had a right to call me kin comes alive again, along with a sense of astonishment that I knew so little about something which had been as vital to my ancestors as it was to these young people. I had not known that big communities in Europe still lived within the Jewish tradition, with the Talmud. I had been unaware of the exclusiveness of their way of life—an exclusiveness to which many wanted to return after six years of concentration camps.

On the shores of Lake Windermere, the Sabbath was strictly upheld, and in the early grey morning mist, the figures of boys with caps on their heads could be seen hurrying to prayers and to lessons with the Rabbi.

For these genuine Orthodox youths, it was a matter of course that they should choose the hostel which the Rabbinate had prepared for them when they had to decide where to go next. The camp in Windermere, unsuitable as accommodation for the winter, was to be closed in November, so the three hundred had to be split up into smaller groups for which hostels all over the country were being prepared. It was left to the boys and girls to choose which one they wanted to go to. Soon a grouping took place, in which initially the individual's attitude towards religion or Zionism seemed to be decisive.

The staff were led by a thoroughly liberal man, who tried to impress on us that the least we could do for the young people was to give them a fair picture and as free a choice of different ways of life as possible. It was hard to carry this attitude through among a staff recruited in one part from the Jewish clergy, in another from the Zionist Youth Alia and other Zionist organisations. There was a sharp conflict of opinion as to what was best for our charges and the young and enthusiastic partisans of this or that group felt it was their duty to see that as many of the boys and girls as possible should decide to follow each of them respectively. I remember feeling very worried about this at the time, but the boys and girls, astute and experienced as they were, mostly avoided the struggle within the community. Many of the staff fought a bitter fight. The liberals were worried, but the boys and girls kept aloof, and changed their minds constantly, according to whether the current leader in Windermere to whom they had become attached was going to this or that hostel, whether this or that friend was going here or there, or whether a locality was situated near enough a town to provide them with the possibility for frequent visits to a cinema, etc.

Almost all of them had been introduced to Zionism in Poland or inside the concentration camps. Palestine was to them the only land where Jews were not persecuted. Their conviction about this was simple and deeply rooted. Their impressions of the friendliness of the English population were of course important, but, as in other instances where emotions were involved, logical conclusions were slow to be considered, if they were taken into account at all. Their impressions of the persecution of their race were not easily wiped out. They were convinced that Jews were being persecuted all over the world, despite being objective and realistic when giving evidence about their personal experiences. They had, for example, no use for the wholesale and much practised slogan, all Germans are bad people, which they now encountered. They argued against this, saying, 'Oh, there are all kinds, there were some nice men and women among the SS...' and they would describe how this or that man or woman guard gave them a Christmas present, or helped them with bits of food and protected them. These pieces of reality had left them with the impression that there were good and bad Germans. It was to be expected, also, that their experiences of goodwill which they found in England would be registered and considered.

Though they had their own opinion of the facts they had witnessed, it would have been impossible to expect them to express themselves as individuals in cases where the group took a stand which would have brought them into opposition with whatever the political, religious or racial outlook of this particular group happened to be. Their loyalty easily became charged with intense aggression and when reinforced by the group, knew no bounds or reason. This is best illustrated by the following incident.

Four boys were living in one of the huts with older boys who were of mixed German and Jewish origin. They were between twelve and fourteen years old, so too old to be with the other 'kids', but too few to be kept in a separate group. After a while we got the impression that they felt persecuted by their hut-mates. We had no proof, and it was hard to get a definitive statement from any of them as they were apparently afraid to talk about it. Then it all came to a head.

One Sunday morning, I took the four boys to the service in the Anglican church in Windermere. One of them had asked to go, the others had joined him, and I had decided to go with them as they were obviously afraid to go alone.

Before this, I had met John, one of the four, at about five in the afternoon when I had finished work in the art room. He had been standing alone at a crossroads and asked me the time. A quarter of an hour later, when I passed again, he was still there, obviously waiting for someone, and again he wanted to know the time. I asked him why he was waiting.

'For a girl,' he said. For a big girl from the village who had said that she would meet him at five o'clock and go with him to the cinema. He did not know her name, and could give only a very vague description, but he had spoken to her the day before and wanted to go on waiting.

I kept myself busy in the next hut where I could keep watch through the window. No girl came. He stood and waited until it was time to go for dinner.

The next day, he was there at the same time, clearly for the same purpose. When I passed him after I had finished work, I asked him whether he had seen the girl in the meantime. He had not. He looked very miserable and I asked if he would like to go to the cinema with me, but he refused. I then suggested he could take the bus and still catch up with the boys who had left to go to the cinema a while ago. He refused to do that as well and explained that he did not like to be with the other boys. He gave as his reason the fact that his brother and the two other little ones had been beaten up the night before by the bigger ones. When I asked why, he said, 'Because we are not Jews,' adding, 'We are frightened of them.'

I asked what religion he was, and he said he did not know. He only knew that he was not a Jew. I told him I was not a Jew either. He wanted to know what I was, and whether I went to church on Sundays. I told him that I did not, but I asked whether he would like to go. His face lit up and he said he would. We agreed to go together on the next Sunday. He immediately wanted to know if the three other boys could go as well if they wanted to. The next day he introduced his friends to me and the excursion to the church in Windermere was fixed between us.

The weather was beautiful on Sunday. When we set off, I saw the boys were wearing their best suits and were clean with well-combed hair. A hundred yards from the gateway, the boys showed me a secret path they knew which led us through the woods up the hill. We had to climb over a fence and through a hedge. Whether they wanted to use this secret path because of their delight in secrecy, or from the wish not to be seen by the rest of the community, I don't know, but probably a bit of both.

I had only told other people about taking the four boys to church at the last minute, as I was not sure whether the boys would really turn up. I had not meant to keep it a secret, even if I could have done, but I thought that whatever their attitude, it was good for our Jewish boys and girls to see that other creeds were taken by us as seriously as theirs.

During that walk through the sunlit woods, one of the boys started to ask the names of the trees—a pine, a beech, an oak and a chestnut. They did not know any these names and learnt them eagerly. The first boy slipped his hand into mine, another did the same from the other side, and so we walked to church.

When we were close, one of them said anxiously, 'How do we behave inside? What will we have to do?'

I told them I did not know the ways of Anglican church services but we could watch what other people did and would copy them. I could see they were in an extremely happy and festive mood. During the service they watched and followed the ceremony attentively.

As we walked back, through the woods again, they told each other about old memories of visits to mass with their families at Christmas. One said he remembered everything. Another picked a small bunch of wildflowers.

I do not know what happened during the afternoon, or who started talking about our visit to church, but by suppertime it was common knowledge. I had expected our visit would upset some of them and was prepared for some signs of disapproval. I hoped it would bring the tension and the hostility under which the four boys suffered into the open and might help to clarify the underlying conflict through action. They did indeed give this sign, if you can call their behaviour that evening by so modest a name.

After a supper which was accompanied by even more noise than usual, the wildest among the big boys attacked, not me, but the four churchgoers and the other small 'mixed' children, as if they had committed a major crime. The aggression against this minority rang out among the huts in words and tone identical in all probability to that used against them by the SS. We had a chance to see them enjoying their turn at behaving ruthlessly as the brutal majority. They called the younger boys, who, a few months previously had shared their misery in the camps, by names which indicated they saw them as associates of the Nazis. A boy of twelve was told he had 'killed my mother'. I was present when this happened. Within a few seconds some twenty big boys seemed to be about to lose all power of reasoning and their pent-up desire for revenge was about to burst bounds. A wild struggle ensued. We tried to pick up the younger ones out of the bundle of wrestling bodies to rescue them. Stones were thrown, but luckily a weekend guest, the husband of our camp doctor, a Zionist, addressed them in Yiddish, and I think this was decisive in preventing the worst, so we managed to get the victims quickly out of the way.

We then separated the most excited ones from the others and walked them up and down the lanes, having a long and initially over-excited talk with them. For a while, it was in the balance as to whether they would be ready to discuss things or would let themselves be completely overcome by the urge for violent action. I remember being pleased that the boys had already sufficient confidence in us and interest in what we would say to prefer a discussion to the continuation of the battle. Above all, loud as they might have been, there were very few fighters among them, and very many talkers.

They were certainly unafraid, but they enjoyed the verbal settling of the dispute and I think they preferred it to settling the argument by force. There had been quite a few occasions already in which we had argued well, holding discussions and 'brain trusts' with them in which there was plenty of opportunity to hear each other's opinions on philosophical, political and religious questions, and in which they learnt how to attack or defend each other without resorting to violence. Of course, it was a different thing to meeting one's opponent in debate to having to calm down a group of young boys in whom they thought they had found a legitimate target for their aggression, with which they were naturally still full to the brim. Yet walking up and down between the huts with them, the doctor found the right words and they were open to his arguments. By talking to them individually, he allowed us to help them become reasonable and calmer.

My initial impulse to take the boys to church was criticised by most of my colleagues. I still think it was an act which, although it upset some of the other boys, was a measure which like so many others they had a right to expect from us, by which I mean the right to be treated as normal people. If they reacted abnormally to normal happenings, it was our duty to help them to re-adjust. If I had refrained from taking the boys to church, the remaining children would have been able to exert the same power of intimidation towards others from which they had suffered so much and had so intensely resented as victims. This would have done them far more harm than being hateful and shouting and being aggressive for a short while. Even if they had caused more severe harm, I would have still counted it a good thing for them to hear our point of view on this occasion, and I think they profited by it.

Another feature of their behaviour was very clear at Windermere: the strong feeling for the group as a unit. We got the impression that it was not simply that the group made decisions, but that as a group they experienced, wished, enjoyed and suffered everything. They spoke of themselves as we. Knowing them better, as I do now, I can give an explanation for this besides the obvious ones. It was not just because they needed the support of larger numbers because of their insecurity and because they were accustomed to the 'group-life', but also that they needed the additional superficial intensity which came through the sharing of emotions with others, because their own emotions had been so blunted. Excitable and emotional as they seemed to be, I learnt to accept the statement which I have heard so frequently since, made by them on so many occasions, that they could not feel anymore.

The group on the one hand provided them with a situation in which the individual was sheltered by the mere presence of the others from exhibiting personal emotions, so that their emotional impotence need not become apparent, and on the other, it gave them the opportunity of experiencing and expressing all forms of mass hysteria as a substitute for true emotion.

We three hundred together at that time therefore meant much to them. Although they had not all shared the same concentration camp, but only started life as a unit in Prague where they had assembled for one transport (in Theresienstadt they had lived in two separate houses), the feeling was still intense, accentuated by communal responses of the kind they had learnt to follow under the Nazi regime.

There was also the singing. They sang together at every possible or impossible occasion. Hearing them sing when they had to wait, when they walked together, as an introduction to every kind of new activity, you got the impression they wanted to be comforted by the feeling of increased strength which comes with being one with a great multitude, of joining voices with many others. On walks, they marched; they did not stroll.

A few weeks after their arrival, this incessant singing decreased. We even found them engaged in a kind of singing match in which different small parties were busy singing different songs simultaneously. A new kind of 'war of the singers' was being fought for supremacy in tone and volume over the others, not to the artistic improvement of the performance, but to the delight of the rest of us, who saw in it a sign of their growing confidence in smaller groups, if not yet in the individual.

The answering 'as one man' had stopped.

A few of them were starting to make useful contacts within the surrounding English families. One made friends with the estate cobbler and was in his house more than in our hut. Another spent time with a family who had a daughter aged sixteen who liked the boy and who had introduced him to her parents. They allowed his daily visits and were considering adopting him, but, after long consideration, the boy turned this down, preferring to stay with his friends. In this case, 'friends' meant the other boys who had shared his life in concentration camp, who were the Polish-Jewish boys and girls with whom he had come from Theresienstadt. For many 'my friends' were precisely that. But some had one special friend. I often wondered what these friendships really were. We respected them, but watched them carefully, as we realised they were more than just the casual friendships between youngsters who had shared their adolescent years and become attached to each other because of a fleeting sympathy favoured by proximity and the wish to expand. These friendships were more important and were of a different stature. They had grown out of unbearable loneliness, they were loaded with severe exclusiveness and with experiences of a forbidding kind, they dragged a net of secrecy along whereby a friend could easily become entangled and turned into a victim. Though they must have been of immeasurable value as the children grew, these intense friendships became a tie with the past and sometimes a danger to the possibilities which a new life in freedom could offer.

Last, but not least, you had to keep in mind how utterly new every single item in the daily life of the boys and girls must have been, and how impossible therefore it was for them to make decisions without knowing what would be involved or expected. The Orthodox ones were in the most familiar surroundings comparatively speaking and, in this respect, their choices held less risk; but even among them there was a certain amount of indecision, and most of the others were easily swayed, making firm decisions one day with the greatest insistence, and another, declining the idea in the light of a new factor, or even an old one.

Most of the Polish boys and girls had come from Orthodox homes. All shades of religious practice were represented among them. I am sure there were deeply religious youngsters among them who clung to the beliefs of their childhood and their parents in all sincerity, though I quite frequently heard assertions by others, equally sincere, that nobody who had gone through years of concentration camps could remain religious.

These were the considerations which weighed on their minds. The people with whom the decision ultimately rested had be aware of these, as well as other factors of which the boys were not conscious, such the suitability of the new locality for school, trade or profession which could be taken up, bearing in mind their physical health.

Sixteen boys and two girls, for example, had had to go to a sanatorium for special supervision and treatment, because they were found to be suffering from slight lung lesions. Luckily most of them were extremely mild cases, probably due to inhalation of small particles while working in quarries and factories. Some new ones joined them from the later transports. More than half, in the meantime, had left the sanatorium and re-joined their comrades having lost all traces of their previous injuries and illnesses.

Eighty of the first three hundred were ordered by the doctor to live for a few more months under special conditions because their fitness was so poor. They were still suffering from the effects of either extreme starvation or typhus, often both.

I have so far talked mostly about boys because my work at Windermere brought me into contact with far more boys than girls. The boys were so much the majority, it meant the camp gave the impression of being a boys' camp. A few pairs of brothers and sisters were with us, and they kept together. There were also friendships between some of the boys and girls, but on the whole, the girls kept to themselves more than would have been expected. Some of the boys spoke badly of the girls.

They had witnessed how some women and girls had sold sex in exchange for food from the guards or troops after liberation, and the boys had therefore concluded that all girls sell themselves.

During their stay in the concentration camps, boys and girls had been kept strictly apart. They were so starved and exhausted by hard labour, so preoccupied with finding themselves extra bits of food, that lack of the opposite sex had not been an issue for them. In the ghettoes, things had been different, and the sexes mixed freely, but our young people had left the ghettoes at a very early age, when they were still children. We had the impression they were backwards in their sex development rather than the opposite. Hardly any of them talked about sexual experiences.

A second reception centre, similar to that at Windermere, started in November 1945 and took in a hundred and fifty children. More came to England, Scotland and Ireland, until by 1946, seven hundred had arrived.

The latter contingents consisted mostly of Czechs and Hungarians, which probably explains the different impression which the later groups gave. The Poles had suffered since 1939, the Czechs for about two years, and the Hungarians for only approximately one year, so it was among the Poles that the striking type of the 'survivor' was more developed and distinctive. Whether this was due to their longer training in survival, or the increasingly rigid selection which from month to month and year to year did its gruelling work more and more thoroughly, or whether it was an innate quality of those Polish-Jewish children, I could not say.

In contrast to the Poles, where the proportion between boys and girls was one to four, among the Czechs and Hungarians it was about equal. This was because in the last part of the war, the scarcity of manpower for the war industry had become so great for the Nazis that many more girls were employed on hard labour tasks, and consequently managed to leave Auschwitz alive, in contrast to the time when the Polish families had met their doom.

Before I close the Windermere chapter, I must make one more statement.

By holding up the magic mirror of my writing, I can see the change my own features underwent since that first night in August, when I thought I could not bear the realisation of a world, my world, the world I lived in, the world I was responsible for, being guilty of such cruelty and misery inflicted upon children. By the end of the year, through trying to help these children to adapt themselves, I learnt to adapt myself, to re-adjust my claims on a reality which seems to lag so much behind the most modest wishes, but which had unexpectedly shown in the features of these children an image of much promise. After the first three months, the following things dawned upon me: that they need not pity, but steady interest; no promises, but a rigid promptness in the execution of plans; and not protection, but readiness to help.

Part 2

The Survivors

In March 1946 I was asked if I would teach eleven of the girls in the camp who were settled in one of the hostels among other refugee youngsters who had spent the entire war or longer there. These girls had arrived only six weeks earlier and were not part of the Windermere group.

This brings me to a description of the work which I said at the start was the reason for my writing this book. The response of the girls to the teaching went far beyond my expectations and revealed such possibilities for helping them that I was keen to share my experiences with other people interested in and concerned with our young friends. The group of girls gave their consent to the publication of our work, though their names, of course, have been changed.

To give a true impression of what we did together I will have to quote myself frequently and extensively. I can see no way of avoiding this, no other way of showing the methods I used, or the girls' responses and the amount we covered.

Reproducing much of the lesson content with the help of my notes will, I think, be the best way to describe the eleven girls with whom I worked.

Their past, their efforts to make up for what they had missed, their difficulties, their strengths and weaknesses were remarkable enough; but in my eyes, this alone would not justify this publication, which by the nature of its material must be very personal. To have undergone these experiences was hard enough for them, so I needed to be convinced that I was doing no harm by publicising both their suffering and the actions they were forced to take due to the most abnormal of circumstances to ensure their survival. At the beginning, I had been certain it would be wrong to expose their tragedy. Later I decided it was my duty to tell of their victorious struggle.

Those among us who had the task of teaching the young people, had the most gratifying of all the jobs, but nobody could give them back their parents or homes. To try to establish substitutes in a situation which was bound to be of short duration would have been wrong and upsetting. How much security could we offer them, even in the ordinary sense, so long as their future was tied up with the politics practised by the different nationalities and parties in Palestine? And not only in Palestine. Nobody can feel secure if they are dependent upon charity, yet it seemed to me that what these victims of catastrophe needed more than anything else was a new sense of security. The girls had lost all sense of direction in both a physical and emotional sense. We knew that the greatest need when leaving a concentration camp, even for an adult, was to know that the fact that you were saved and alive was important to at least one other person in the wide world. This one other person could point the compass in the right direction for their ship to be steered

43

across the high seas, but without this, any further voyage would be directionless. We could not give them this vital one person, but we could help these young people find roughly where they stood in space and time; geographically, historically, physically and biologically.

I had no doubt that the strongest feeling they had was that of loss; both of having lost, and of being lost. A poem written by a seventeen-year-old Polish boy expresses this well. When he wrote this poem, he had only been in England six months, so his knowledge of English was only six months old. This accounts for the errors of vocabulary and grammar but does not explain his astonishing poetic mastery of the language.

Lost
Everyone, when born
starts a walk across their life
from a little boy, until they get bread, salt and family knife
[A Jewish saying, indicating adulthood.]

For some it is a nice walk,
for some it is bad,
for some long and
for others short and sad.

But everyone is going on
the way of their life and fate,
and nobody arrives at the goal
because always it is too late.

Yes, I was, and am also—
I can remember a very nice time—
but I had to go cross a wood,
A DEFENDANT WITHOUT A CHINK...

A wood, a dark wood, where
there were wild animals inside.
I did not want to go there,
My spirit and heart were afraid,

But I must go into the wood,
A strong arm stretched out for me,
wild animals attacked me, but I go...
I must find the freedom's key.

At once there came a big animal
put the claw to my heart,
tore a piece out, I fell
and the blood flowed from me.

I am like a fly in a cobweb,
over me stands my host,
I dip my hand in my blood
and write that word, 'LOST'.

There came a fire to the wood…
on my heart lies a stone.
The wood is destroyed
and the freedom has won

And the rays of freedom had made me strong.
I stood up and went away from my host…
a stone always lies on my heart
and I always remember the bloodword, 'LOST'.

A nine-year-old boy drew a picture which could have been given the same title. He took great pains to draw two little figures, caught up in a net. It seemed to me to express an identical feeling to the poem. The two boys belonged to different groups and did not know each other.

Attempts at orientation

I am not a trained teacher. My education stopped at Matriculation after six years of attending a Lyceum in Vienna. I have lived in many different parts of the world, including years in the Far East, periods in Germany, Holland, France, the USA, as well as the war years which I spent in England. I have undertaken different kinds of work in different countries, but I have not been systematically trained, or widely educated. To be told to teach 'all subjects except English' to girls of sixteen and over was a big ask for a person like myself. The scarcity of teachers was the only reason I found myself in this position, and also the only reason I dared to take the job. I knew nothing of any profession other than painting, but I was asked to teach these girls general school subjects, so my work would contribute to the second part of the programme.

I had one weekend to prepare myself, and speculated that although my own knowledge was patchy, it had been sufficient so far to provide me with the skills to follow more than one occupation, to enjoy meeting and talking to many kinds of people, and to enjoy reading many kinds of books. It had sufficed to give me a good enough life. If I succeeded—and that would be the best possible outcome—in sharing with the girls all I knew, it should be enough for them as well. On the other hand, I knew that to teach you had to be sure of what you wanted to convey, and I had the feeling there would be many gaps in my knowledge which I would not discover until confronted by them. To give me a direction to follow in my own instruction as well as in the actual teaching, I thought it would be helpful and would simplify matters if I were to start at the very beginning, eons ago, and let things develop from there. Working this way, we would learn about events in the correct historical order. Thought and knowledge would develop in the most orderly fashion if we followed a linear itinerary.

I spent Saturday morning at one of London's biggest bookshops asking advice from the assistant in the educational department and went home with four books with the help of which I prepared my first lessons. These books were: Man and his World by James Mainwaring; The Marvels and Mysteries of Science (Oldham Press); a textbook of biology for elementary schools; and a book of mathematics.

These books provided me with exactly what I needed. They contained enough material and were arranged in such a way that they could be used as a simple framework, yet they had enough scope to support all I could teach the girls about the world in the few months available.

One other factor made me decide on this approach. I knew the girls had come from many different types of school, which they had attended for different lengths of time, so I had to take their varying levels of education into account and cater for all. From my experiences in Windermere, I knew I had to catch their attention in the very first lesson and hold it or there would be no pupils in my class for the second. The very beginning of things holds a fascination for everybody—for adolescents, perhaps, even more than for anyone else.

Having enjoyed this start together, I would be free to take varied paths, leading in all directions, to find out which they would prefer to follow. I intended to teach the changes our world has undergone, the history of its inhabitants and the development of knowledge about matter, through a co-ordinated scheme of both timescale and causation.

You could argue that it was a waste of time to teach the Stone Age, the Crusades, the laws of gravity, the structure of the universe and the atom, and the geography of Central Africa to a group of young girls who had lost literally everything, who must be suffering from worries of the greatest magnitude, and for whom it was paramount to learn a trade or a profession to gain at least material independence, but there were two counter-arguments in favour of a few months of educational work. One was purely logistical. Places in training colleges were hard to come by and enrolment could only happen at the start of the term. Secondly, giving the girls a higher level of education was considered justified. Learning a trade would help them gain material independence, but they also needed help to become more independent in their outlook. These were the tasks of rehabilitation. The necessary period of waiting before they could be moved on again was useful for both purposes.

I will be quoting from the notes I made immediately after, and sometimes during, the lessons. It is a pity that in many cases I had to translate and could not reproduce what the girls had said in the original Yiddish German, an exceedingly expressive language.

Intensive work starts

The warden of the hostel in North London where the girls were placed had asked for their removal. My arrival every morning was accepted by her as a last resort. During my first interview with her, she had described the girls to me as very difficult, unwilling to take part in the life of the community, and resentful of even the slightest suggestion for co-operation in household duties. They were unpunctual and untruthful, they made demands with great vehemence, but they were never prepared to do their share. They were quarrelsome, fighting among each other and with the older inmates of the hostel. They had upset the discipline in the house and were undoing the warden's work of many years. They were very rude and often impolite. In short, they were unsatisfactory in every respect.

That was the description I had of my future pupils. I do not remember precisely how I was introduced to the girls, but I well remember the inquisitive looks, the loud chatter which did not let up when I came in the room, and which gave it a cynical and disagreeable atmosphere rather than the jolly one I had hoped for when standing among them for the first time.

I sat down and started our first lesson by saying: 'Let us start at the very beginning. If you like, I can describe what the experts who have studied the subject think was there at the very beginning: before men, before animals, before plants or even mountains and rivers. Before the earth was there at all. Just what existed at the very start. Then I can tell you what happened next in the order in which scientists think it happened. That way, we can find out what you think is interesting, and what you would like to learn more about; what you do not yet know.'

Here they interrupted me with, 'We know nothing,' and chattered on in Polish, which I could not understand. When they had quietened down again, they agreed we could try to start in the way I had suggested.

On that first Monday morning and throughout the week we talked about the universe—its size, distances, space, orbits, the order of the solar system and the changes of the surface of the earth. By Thursday we reached the appearance of the first forms of life. The girls were interested when I described these phenomena and showed them pictures and graphs out of the books. They enjoyed marvelling at it all and did not resent being dragged along into infinitely vast space.

On Thursday morning, I reported on the first signs of life. I had just started giving a description of fossils and the most probable forms of subsequent development when I was interrupted by Maria, a Hungarian girl of sixteen, the most aggressive among them, who, in a rather haughty and rude tone, asked me how I could prove what I was telling them.

This very sensible question had not been asked before. When stars exploded, when the Sun gave birth to planets, when nothing had cooled off and matter as we know it had been born from gas and fire, they had listened with apparent interest, giving no sign that they doubted for a moment that what they were told was true. But when we reached a point, still millions of years away in the past, yet a vista at the end of which they could recognise their own outline, though I had not mentioned it, and we were talking about the matter of which they were made—then they wanted proofs.

Had they up to now been listening to what I was describing as if I were telling a tale, interesting but not directly concerning them? And was it only when I mentioned life that what I said gained an importance which made it worth their knowing if there were facts behind the stories? That was the most likely explanation, though I thought I detected a different sounding note in the question. It had been asked in Maria's characteristic haughty tone, the subtext being: do not think you can tell us anything about life.

I answered by saying I would like to show them the fossils at the Natural History Museum. We arranged to go there the following morning.

We met at South Kensington tube station. They arrived half an hour late in the pouring rain. When we got to the museum gates, we found them shut with a board saying, 'Until further notice'. I asked a porter what that meant, and he replied it would re-open in about a year's time.

We still managed to get in. By pure chance, a gentleman was just coming out of the gates into the pouring rain. I told him who the girls were and why we had come. He was a scientist on the staff and helped us obtain entry. Not only that, the head of the fossils departments took the trouble to take us round himself to explain the exhibits and the development of plant and animal life to the girls, who were clearly fascinated. They asked questions and discussed what they had heard, and our guide was fascinated in turn. He found them 'so philosophical' and 'different from the English young people we see here'.

He gave up his whole morning to our visit and at the end offered to arrange with some of his colleagues to be our guides through the other departments on future visits to the museum. I was only too glad to accept this offer, so on the three following Fridays, we enjoyed being shown around the different parts of the museum.

Each time the girls were thrilled with what they saw and declared the visit to be the best yet. The lecturers were struck by the thoroughness with which they went from one exhibition case to another and studied what was inside. It did not occur to the girls to skip any of it.

Our morning lessons at the hostel now included quite a variety of subjects. The idea had always been that I should do my teaching in English, but the girls had only arrived in England two months previously and hardly knew any of the language as yet. I soon realised that if I wanted them to understand what I said, I would have to use German, certainly at first. Even then it was difficult enough for some of them to follow, because German, being a foreign language for all, also presented difficulties.

They were a mixed group of six Poles and five Hungarians, and all received English lessons from an English teacher in the afternoon, so I made light of the fact that I was teaching them in German. I considered it more important for them to understand what I was teaching than to practise their English.

The warden of the hostel complained that there were bitter fights going on between the two groups, there was a constant friction and strain, and certainly, in the morning during lessons, they often quarrelled, shouting at each other excitedly in a language I could not understand.

We had reached a place in the history of our globe where the human species had populations everywhere, so it was easy to see that there would be controversy about the different ways of life different people would choose. This led to heated and disorderly attempts by the girls to state their opposing opinions. I stopped the arguments by suggesting we should have a proper discussion in the style of a formal debate, with rules, a speaker for the motion, a speaker against, and a chairman. They agreed enthusiastically. One of them, Miriam, was elected to propose Communism as the right way of life. The opposition was represented by Susan, who proposed the democratic way.

We had our debate on the first warm day of spring in the back garden of the hostel. The girls exhibited great enthusiasm and put forward strong arguments both for and against the case. They elected me as their chairman, but I refused the honour because I was sure they would want to hear my opinion on this issue, and I thought they had a right to hear it. I wanted to be free to support the opposition which tallied with my views and was by far in the minority.

The pro-Communists had 'as it is done in Russia' as a broad description of how they would like to see things done, but as well as this general statement, they produced some sincere arguments taken from their longing for justice and equality. The individualists shared in this, but they were against 'as it is in Russia' as they had experienced some of this after liberation and had not liked it. They wanted to feel free and did not want other people to decide for them how and where they should live. All of them planned to go to Palestine, the pro-Communists to live together in a shared and protected settlement, the others as private citizens. The meeting was noisy as they were speaking with raised voices, but it had cleared the atmosphere.

I did not speak much during the debate. Towards the end they asked me what I thought about it all. I told them I personally preferred the democratic way of life, but that I knew very little of Communism. I thought both ways had an ideal society in mind, which, if looked at closely, was not so very different and could work well in either case if people were well-disposed towards each other.

'Better,' was Miriam's reply to this.

So, the difference in the method of achieving this, which was all I could find at the heart of it all, would perhaps not matter quite so much.

What it means to them

For the first month we heard about the earliest civilisations appearing, growing, making contact, fighting and conquering each other. We learnt the geography of the parts of the world where this took place. We did arithmetic and learnt some basic botany and zoology. We were busy with the laws of gravitation and started on the principles of waves, rays, heat and electricity. They had to use their imaginations. First, they had to grasp how impossible it was to imagine the vastness of the universe. I wondered if it would have a calming effect to know about the laws of physics that existed out there, and whether it would increase their sense of security to imagine enormous distances, compared to which the self would shrink into an infinitely tiny entity. Would this knowledge be a relief to people who took themselves more seriously than is normal? I would not have questioned this had I not often heard sighs coming from my young pupils when we talked about this subject; the sort of sighs of relief you give when you learn of a great secret. Perhaps it helped to shift the burden of suffering and alleviated some of the pressure on their personal world to see that there are innumerable centres of gravity. During these lessons, I caught my first glimpses of how readily those strong young creatures would catch hold of anything that could help them to improve, to become healthier, to become normal. They absorbed their lessons the way parched land absorbs rain. The hours we spent together were often beautiful as they expanded, loosened up, and became calmer.

The following incident though, which happened much later, throws a curious light on this period. Maria, who was the one who had expressed her doubts in my first lessons and was one of the cleverest girls, had discovered she had a half-brother alive in Budapest. Three months after we started our lessons, she received a book from him, a Hungarian translation of James Jean's book which used the same photos and descriptions of the same astronomical phenomena we had worked through together. She had apparently received the book because of an enthusiastic letter she had sent him describing her new knowledge. She was delighted with this gift and read it aloud to her friends, showing me the beautiful pictures if they were completely new to her. This puzzled me. I showed her the identical pictures in our book, to which, incidentally, James Jean had contributed the part on astronomy, and reminded her we had covered all of this two months ago.

'I remember something of the kind,' she said, 'but surely then it meant something else. I have completely forgotten all of it.'

At the time it must have meant much to her, or she would not have written to her brother in such a way to make him send the book to her. Yet two months later, she had 'forgotten nearly all of it'. Why? She had been the most interested person, taking the biggest share in all the questions and discussions. If she hardly remembered anything, would the others have remembered even less? What could cause that? Had the material been too new? Could it not be fixed to anything in their experience, and had it therefore fallen through some gap and disappeared? Or was this failure to remember similar to the amnesia which accompanies the associations which can bring emotional relief in psychiatric work, so that when the beneficial result is achieved, the how and wherefore is completely forgotten? I wondered if their acquaintance with an image of a wider world had been accompanied by so many emotions and relief that nothing connected with it had been seen as intellectual work, but instead as belonging to the emotional side of things. Had it been compartmentalised separately from intellectual knowledge, disappearing from the list of goods held in the mental larder, and used for another purpose to strengthen the structure of the being? In Maria's words: 'But surely then it meant something else?'

When I started teaching them mathematics, I found they were especially keen on the subject. They loved working through long and complicated calculations with brackets. Routine and seemingly boring repetition appeared to have an attraction for them. Through it, they gained the satisfaction of finding the hidden solution, clear, undisputable and neat, the sort of thing only mathematical problems could provide. They never tired of this work, and always wanted to carry on when we had to stop at the end of the morning.

Lena's story

It was not until the fifth week that the girls started to show that they looked upon me not just as a teacher, but also as a human being who they might like to get to know better.

The young people in Windermere had behaved so differently. This might have been because the girls' stay at the hostel was their third placement within two months of arriving in England, so they had become wary of talking to people. Perhaps, also, now that the liberation was further behind them, the urge to tell strangers about their experiences had spent itself. It could also have been that my style of teaching, the telling of impersonal facts and events far away in space and time, had satisfied them sufficiently for their morning's activity, so it had not occurred to them to discuss personal issues. They were fascinated by, and proud of, what they learnt, as was confirmed to me by the warden who told me the girls were discussing and talking about their new knowledge during meals and at other times.

I shall pause my descriptions of the group work here to record two personal histories, first Lena's, and then the story of Maria, because during this period these were the two who showed most clearly that they needed my help in a direct and personal way.

Lena was the only one who had not profited at all from my teaching. Her German was poor, and she was so self-absorbed at first that she could not direct her attention to me, and neither could I catch it. Her unhappiness among the other girls meant that for a long time she behaved and was treated as an outsider. She moved with an unnatural and affected grace and talked with difficulty due to sheer shyness. One other feature distinguished her from the others. Her only means of self-expression was through pictures, so there is no trace of her when the group experiences are described. But her story goes here on record.

As the situation in Transylvania (her home) had become more and more dangerous for Jews, her mother had sent her and her little sister to an aunt in Budapest, hoping they would be safer in a bigger town than the village where everyone knew they were Jews. Lena's parents and her sisters who stayed at home disappeared into Poland's camps. Lena knew none of the details. She was taken on the street in Budapest one day by the Gestapo, was imprisoned, then deported to Auschwitz. From there, the path of her suffering was similar to that of the others. Her youngest sister also disappeared.

When I arrived on the morning of the 10th of April, Lena told me she had brought herself a new dress the previous day and asked me whether I would like to see it. She brought it to the classroom at my request.

The next morning, a few of the girls attacked her in my presence. I have forgotten the incident that precipitated this, but she was accused of being 'no comrade'. They told me nobody liked her, nobody wanted to share a room with her, and she thought she was better than the rest of them. Lena blushed and smiled with embarrassment but said nothing.

I told them that I was sure Lena had reasons for her apparently antisocial manner. They immediately interrupted me.

'Yes, she thinks she is better than us.'

I told them I had the impression Lena was not happy, but as she obviously preferred to be by herself, the girls ought to respect that wish. There was nothing to resent. Anybody was free to live and share company or not, after his or her own choices. There were no further reactions from the girls. Lena still smiled blankly.

The warden confirmed what the girls had said. She also told me that immediately after her arrival in London, Lena had asked for an interview at the head office. She had expressed her wish to see a plastic surgeon because she wanted her nose changed. This was refused. Since then, she had returned at least once a week on the same errand, imploring the office staff to help her to change her profile. She was obsessed with the idea.

Her nose was a genuine disfigurement. It was very pronounced, overlong and drooping, spoiling her otherwise delicate and pretty features. She must have suffered severely as a result and would have been over-conscious of her appearance in a country where the Nazis treated people with accentuated facial features, unless Germanic ones, as special targets for their brutality. Her nose would have been a constant reminder of what had happened. In her eyes, it may even have been partly responsible for her sufferings.

I watched her for a few days. She never passed a mirror without stopping to look into it, arrange her hair, and twist round in an attempt to see more of her pretty figure. She accompanied her conversation with an excessive number of wavy gestures with her very pretty hands.

I had a talk with her in which she confirmed the warden's words. When I asked whether she really thought noses mattered so much, she said she did. I told her I thought that they did not, because a nose could not change with the expression on a face, and that what people really observed about each other was their expressions, as this showed the personality, which the profile did not. The eyes and the mouth changed with emotion and so altered the face, showing who you were. They mattered far more than the nose, which did not change the smallest part of an inch, whether one was happy or sad, or in a grumpy or pleasant mood.

She said, stolidly, 'My nose is very ugly, and I want it changed.'

I took her to one of the leading plastic surgeons. The doctor wanted to know how long Lena had had this idea of having her nose changed by an operation.

'When I was still a small girl at home, my mother promised me that when I was grown up, a doctor would change my nose,' she said.

'What kind of a nose would you like to have?' he asked.

Lena was unable to find the words to describe what she wanted her nose to look like, so I suggested she draw it.

She took a pencil and made a scribble that looked like this:

}

The doctor nodded and said he understood what she meant. He told her he was happy to change her profile. There was only one snag, and this brought tears to her eyes. She would have to wait three more months.

In the interval between her interview and the operation she became more sociable and even made friends with one of the other girls. She had a very good relationship with me, and started to go to a dressmaking college, which she loved. Things generally improved for her.

When the time for the operation came, it was done and proved very successful. Lena's looks changed so suddenly it was hard to believe. Before, we had felt embarrassed to look at her as she so obviously hated being seen. Many people failed to recognise her after the operation. The pretty dimpled girl, with the friendly uncomplicated expression on her face, whom none of us had noticed before, was very different to the Lena we had known.

On the way back from the nursing home, she sat in the bus and looked out of the window. It was a grey and rainy day. When we passed through Baker Street, not the most attractive of thoroughfares, she opened her hands in a wide gesture and said with a sigh, 'It is all so beautiful.' Her gratitude was intense. She used these words to describe her happiness over and over again, feeling a new life had started for her.

By a happy coincidence, there was a party in the hostel on the evening of her return. She, who had always been a wallflower, danced all night. She had lost all her affectations and was radiantly happy.

I am afraid I have to report on a downside to this happy story. We, who had started to be fond of Lena, found it difficult to accustom ourselves to her new features because, contrary to what I had so boldly stated in my talk with her, a different nose did make a considerable difference, much more so than anyone who had never seen it could realise. This was a new, slightly strange Lena, and we confessed to each other we resented the change.

I am afraid it looked as if Lena herself, a few months later, was suffering again. She did not look well, was depressed, wanted to stop going to college, and seemed at a loose end. I did not know what the matter was, but I would imagine it is a complex experience having one's profile changed. This new state of being good-looking was hard work for her. Something had been lost when the surgeon took away the surplus flesh of her nose. Some real part of Lena had gone, and she needed time to adjust herself to the slightly unreal Lena she had become.

Reality is hard. Fulfilment of the most urgently wished-for desires is not the same as in fairy tales. Even in stories, it is not the princess with the big nose who is simply turned into the princess with the small nose to live happily ever after. There is much suffering to be borne and much patience to be practised before, thanks to the work of her surgeon magician, she can become a beautiful princess.

As I said earlier, Lena took no active part in the lessons. She gave the impression of being a keen person who tries to look as if she is capable of following the lesson, when in reality she knows she cannot, and is afraid she will be found out. Hers was the attitude of an anxious misfit. It was all the more apparent because the others were not ashamed to let me know if they could not understand what I said or when I had been going too fast for them.

When the first drawing lesson was due, in the very first week, Lena had told us that she had been good at painting when she was a child. The first of her pictures— a ghost in a blue dress—took her half an hour to do and gave her great satisfaction. The following week she painted a picture of geese which clearly reflected her mood. Their attitude was aggressive, yet cowering, showing the everywhere-ness of her problem. They were not overwhelmingly big, for then she would have filled her paper with one giant goose, but overwhelmingly there, crowning her world with the misery and aggression expressed through geese and a loveless tree.

She commented on this picture, pointing to the half which was filled with the tree, saying, 'I wanted to paint a girl there, but I could not.'

This was followed by pictures of endless regular rows of hills. They crowded the horizon in browns, greens, mauves and blacks. The eleven girls painted one landscape with extremely steep high mountains in fifty-nine variations over a period of four months. This scene had nothing to do with the flat Polish plains. By the end of our work together, the landscapes were less violently despairing in appearance. I need to stress here that I never made the slightest comment on what was painted, except to use the cliché 'lovely'.

But to go back to Lena's story. There was a break in her stay at the hostel. She accepted an invitation from a family with the possibility of staying there for good, to be adopted at a later date, but she came back after three weeks. She seemed to have enjoyed herself, but nothing came of the placement.

After this break, her pictures showed a few trees of a completely different type from the broomstick kind she had drawn before. They were crowned with balls; the way small children would paint them. A path made an appearance on her pictures at this point, painted either blue or yellow.

While she was painting, and immediately afterwards, she was completely satisfied with her work and admired it naively, whereas the others often complained their paintings were not good enough. Lena had a rapt expression on her face when she looked at her finished pictures and put them up on the mantelpiece for show.

It was striking to observe how much she liked the opportunity to show the pictures she had created. She, who had told me that she hated looking at herself in the mirror (which, however, she did as frequently as possible); she, who went round with an expression on her face of embarrassment about her looks, found these poor ugly empty drawings to be 'reflections of her as surely as the reflection in the mirror'; faultless, beautiful and worth showing. How she must have longed for approbation.

And here I found the other girls being kind to her for the first time. They imitated my appreciation of the pictures. Lena could not get enough of it. She beamed all over and was really happy.

After she had been to see the surgeon, she painted a picture with a little church and steeple and immediately afterwards, on the same morning, the only one she ever did that included people. A knight was riding towards a house with a lit window. She explained the picture illustrated a Hungarian song.

'When the moon shines, the girl dreams of a prince who comes on a white horse.'

The horse in the picture, by the way, is red.

From then on, she stuck to a certain rule and order when she painted. She would produce two pictures each time. The first would be alive, with varying subject matter; while the second always showed the same despairing old rows of hills she had painted at the start.

Among the material which I kept and used for comparison there were two distinct types of 'artist', each with their own strict order of production. The ones similar to Lena started the session with the more complicated picture, the one which seemed to describe 'the weather as it is at the moment' and recorded changes and what was happening at that time. This would be followed with the 'but this is still true, this is not yet forgotten, look at this' picture, which would contain the ever-recurring problem, expressed in an ever-recurring simple symbol.

The other type of artist started with a 'look at it, this I have to say first, then only can I talk about other things' picture, which would be followed with a more varied, saner and richer tale.

Maria's story

The morning after the incident with Lena, the room was tense but exceptionally quiet at the start of lessons. Georgette had a black eye and Maria was absent. She arrived twenty minutes later and at once started butting in with her cynical remarks. These were immediately countered by Gina, with an equal display of temperament. Both girls poured out a shower of abuse in German. This language was used because though Maria was Hungarian and Gina Polish, German swearwords were known to both parties. At least it meant I could follow what it was all about.

Gina accused Maria of wanting to rule like a queen over all the girls in the hostel, not only over her Hungarian subjects, but over the Poles as well. She ended by saying she would not accept being treated by her as she treated her Hungarian friends, she would not be beaten up as Maria had beaten up Georgette, and at the slightest attempt to bully her, Gina would not hesitate to kill Maria, and she would not be the first one whom she had killed either.

Maria was in blazing rage. She lost control of herself and broke into hysterical screams, shouting, 'And I will kill you. I will kill you now if you are impudent with me. You think I won't? You shall see me kill. I shall kill the people, whether one or three, I shall kill them all; the ones who have beaten up my father, I have seen them, and I will kill them. That is all I want to do in life.'

She shook and she screamed, and the others hurled back more abuse.

After a while, I managed to make myself heard. I told them I wanted to say something about Maria. They asked what it was. I told them that if they found Maria difficult to live with peacefully, it was because she was unhappier than the rest of them.

They shouted back, 'No, no, we have all suffered the same, why should she be more unhappy?'

I said I thought it was because, first of all, she was the youngest one here so had lost her parents at an earlier age then they had, and that was harder. Also, for some people, things were harder to bear than for others. All I had seen of Maria showed me she was having a hard time right now. I was very sorry to see her suffer and, if they would only try and help by being nice to her and stop minding so much when she misbehaved, it would help them all because there would be less friction. Their community life would be more peaceful and agreeable.

There were discontented murmurs from nearly all the girls.

Maria, who had been standing, turned and left the room. I went on talking about her for a few minutes in her absence, repeating what I had said, and stressing that I knew they had all suffered.

Ruth, a girl with the looks of a Polish peasant, interrupted and challenged me, saying: 'I had to obey my mother while I was at home. Now that my mother is dead, and I am free, I shall not obey anybody.'

I carried on with the lesson. About half an hour later, the door opened and Maria came in with red and swollen eyes. She put an packet down in front of me. It contained blackboard chalk, and three pencils to give to three of the girls, one of whom was Georgette with the black eye.

A while ago I had complained about the shortage of chalk.

Maria had obviously had a good cry and then gone out to buy these things for us. She had the proverbial Hungarian pride but could allow herself to be humble. At sixteen-years-old, she was very temperamental, with a clear logical mind and a quick laugh. She was very good looking, sparkling with life, a joy to meet and the type of pupil who enlivened every lesson, but occasionally she was in the vilest of tempers, as if soaked in despair and kicking with aggression - just as we had seen then. Sometimes she had the kind of absent-mindedness which gave the impression the person was living elsewhere, though her body was in our presence.

In the hostel she had been the cause of incessant complaints at first. She wandered off by herself, came in at irregular hours and was always late. She took no notice of the house rules and regulations and was uncooperative, haughty, demanding, taking things for granted, rude, and quarrelsome. The list of her faults seemed endless.

During lessons, I was astonished at how much she knew, at the interest she showed and her receptiveness. Her father had been a Hungarian banker and an international chess master. Maria had adored him. Her mother had died before the outbreak of war. Maria had an older half-brother and a younger sister. Her father and the little sister were killed together in Maria's presence.

She had performed an extraordinary feat in Auschwitz by managing to steal away from the crowd the SS Guard had assembled to be exterminated. She had hidden herself in a corner of one of the stores when she heard a search had been organised to find her, but she discovered that everybody else, without exception, would be killed if she was not found.

'I was in great difficulties,' she said in her broken German. 'I did not know whether everybody was to be killed anyhow because of me or what—I did not want other people to die because of me, but I did not want to die either.'

It was no use. She was oh, so hungry. She came out of hiding. On that very day, Auschwitz, which had to function as a labour exchange for unskilled labour as well as extermination centre, received an urgent appeal from one of the German munition factories to immediately send two-hundred and fifty young women and girls to work there. That number was picked out of the thousands of candidates for death and sent to a place near Dresden to work. Maria was among them.

Over the course of several weeks, I got the impression that Maria suffered from a combination of circumstances which made her present life particularly repulsive to her. She resented the fact that the girls around her were from a different background. This was not due to a snobbishness on her part. She was not grading or classifying them, but she missed the intellectual background which she had known at home, the good clothes and the cultured environment in which she had been raised. Even more than that, she resented the fact that she thought she would be expected to stop her education, unable to continue from where she had left off, and fated therefore to slip forever into a different kind of world to the one she and her parents had intended her to have.

Many, many, refugee children and youngsters were in that position, and accepted it gracefully, but Maria was not prepared to be one of them. She was ready to fight for her education and was prepared to work hard.

Another girl who longed to continue learning, with school as a preparation for a university career, was Georgette, who had always wanted to be a doctor. Both girls were well above average intelligence. Georgette showed great integrity and a steady strong mind. I had the impression she might be capable of working hard and achieving her aim. Maria, who was most likely the more intelligent of the two, was gravely handicapped by her unstable and difficult temperament. But I also thought she should have the chance to go back to school, if for no other reason than it meant so much to her as part of her rehabilitation.

The search for a suitable school which would accept them as pupils proved fruitful. The headmistress of the local borough school was ready to see if they would fit in and the two girls started to go there regularly from the beginning of the summer term onwards. They were immensely happy about it. Maria changed from the very first day. Her boisterous, temperamental and enthusiastic side became apparent and she carried everyone along with her with whom she had contact.

The staff and other girls at the school showed all the necessary understanding and patience. After two terms in the age-appropriate class, the girls were doing very well. Where they still fell short and had difficulties will become clear later on.

History

After Easter, when we started up again, we missed the two girls from our little group. The remaining nine were very keen now on their morning's work. Our programme was varied enough, but it felt as if all we were learning was related, as if the whole was really only one subject—that of getting to know what had happened in this world and what there was to be found. It was within this subject that they exercised their minds. When they followed me, they moved through time and space, through concepts of both the infinitely great and the minute. I had not planned to teach like this, but, as I proceeded, I became aware it was happening. The girls were not only ready to work in this way and enjoy it, they were also becoming less rigid and aggressive towards each other; less self-assertive and less noisy during lessons. Their energy was spent, it would seem, not so much in learning in the usual sense, as on increasing their ability to experience. This, due to the nature of their past, took on a highly emotional quality. All they had known of the world so far had been extreme bodily suffering and mental hardship. Good or bad relationships with human beings in whose power they existed had overshadowed anything else they could know of life. Now their personal experiences faded into the background for a while as objective facts became the focus of their attention.

To those readers of this book who happen to be teachers, I must confess I never tested to see how much of what I taught had been taken in by any of the girls, how much had been digested or was in a state to be reproduced. It sufficed if they were interested while the lesson lasted. If you imagine the patchiness of this group's knowledge, magnified by the fact that they were at such different educational levels, and you remember that the period of my tuition was intended to last only a few months, I do not think I can be blamed for treating the task mostly as a journey through the realm of knowledge; an attempt to at least get a bird's eye view of its vastness, while gathering on the way any unexpected fruit I found ripening.

All I did towards fixing in their minds what we had learnt each morning was to dictate to them a short summary in English of everything covered by the end of the session. It gave them the confidence that they could always check up for themselves on what they had learnt, and it was an obvious proof for them that they had learnt something. It was also was an exercise in English and provided them with that subject's particular vocabulary.

So much for my technique, which was of the simplest, the tale-telling kind. 'I went on with the story,' best expresses what we did.

When we reached the Ancient Egyptian and Greek cultures in history, we visited the newly opened British Museum. A large gallery, the only one yet open, contained an extraordinarily well-curated display of the crafts of the ancient world. Greek, Roman, South Sea, early Teutonic and Celtic pottery, glass and metal work of perfect beauty, were all arranged in such a way that you were not overburdened by the number and similarity of the objects but could enjoy each as a significant example of a craft.

The girls were very impressed. Again, their thoroughness in examining every exhibit was striking and most satisfying. We had to go twice because we only managed to see half the room on the first morning. History became their pet subject for a while, so every morning that week, except for Thursday and the Sabbath, we read accounts of ancient history.

I well remember the feeling of happiness these mornings gave me. I was allowed to show these young ones the way people had thought and behaved and struggled and tried to improve and to help, had failed and succeeded, suffered, enjoyed, built and destroyed and fought. I could give them an idea of the complexity of life, of life even at that early stage; the liabilities and the obligations, the changes in importance, the rut of orthodoxy, the power which goes with the priesthood and ritual, the longing for 'the better', the fear of the new, the craving of men to understand and to see order.

Innumerable possibilities sprang from using ancient history as a medium to show how there had always been fights, always been suffering, victims and conquerors, and always people who had tried hard to find a better way of doing things. I tried to get them to see the analogies.

I may have been teaching history, but I used every chance I found in every chapter to help them understand how suffering is a part of all human life, and that changing and creating and doing is another. They should stop seeing their own situation as being burdened with a paralysing weight of uniqueness and should instead consider how everything that happened was linked with everything else, at least historically, even if they could not see that in the present. Human sacrifices, the Roman arena, the persecution of the early Christians, the conquering power behind great religious ideas, the beauty of crafts, the searching thoroughness of the great philosophies, the part that craving for power has played in communities, the importance of the individual, the contagious influence of class—there were innumerable opportunities to show them reality from different points of view. Because they were distant in time, these points of view presented problems which were easier for them to accept in their implications than they would have been had they been closer to home. All this showed them how much there was to know about their world. They felt they had gained knowledge and that made them more contented. I think they must have enjoyed it while we did it.

Yet I am aware that very few of the facts they heard from me stuck in their memories. All they learnt about this or that left only a vague impression in their minds, just as in Maria's failure to recognize that she had already learnt the simple astronomical laws with us. But they all attended the classes keenly, and absenteeism was nil from the third week onwards, proving their continued enjoyment.

I noted what the warden reported about those weeks in my diary. The girls were less loud and more polite. The fights between the two groups, the Poles and the Hungarians, had stopped completely. They were now one group, though they did not mix with the other girls yet. They were not rude any more with the exception of Ruth and her friend Ellen. But they were still as unpunctual as ever and lived their own way, doing whatever they liked, regardless of the house rules.

At about that time, a friend of mine offered to give piano lessons to any girls who were interested. Their reaction to this, their gratitude and keenness, gave me a glimpse of what 'special privileges' meant to these starved creatures. I therefore looked out for as many possibilities as I could find to increase this kind of experience for them, and at the same time I started to feel I could dispense with some of the reserve I had exercised.

In my teaching, I was still sticking strictly to my initial careful approach. With the exception of two occasions—one caused by Lena's troubles and the other by Maria—we had never talked about personal problems in the group. So far, I had only had one private talk, the one with Lena on about her appearance.

Maria was the only one of the girls who had mentioned any details relating to her own experiences—when she talked about her father's death in an outburst of rage. I still knew nothing about any of the rest of them.

Eight weeks after we had first met, on the 7th May, we had just finished a lesson on the persecution of the early Christians, when I said I knew they had undergone similar sufferings and it worried me, as I was growing to know them a little, and to like them, that I did not know more about matters which must be of great importance to them and often on their minds. I told them I would be grateful if they could tell me about such things, to help me to know them better.

'It would be like a lesson on a period in modern history which you could give me for a change,' I said.

'All right,' they said, and, 'Why not?' an exclamation often used by them to indicate full approval.

And so they told me when they had left home and how long they had stayed in ghettoes and concentration camps. They did it in a very detached way, this 'providing me with the dates'.

Another story

The painting period was in the second half of the morning. Anne, who had been a democrat in our political discussion, was a real artist. She produced rich, impressive pictures and said of herself, when I paint, I can tell myself things, it helps. She was nearly always depressed, spoke very rarely, but when she said anything, she addressed it to the paint and showed that she was clever and knew her own mind. She was seventeen and a half years old at this point.

At the end of one morning she lingered on in the room when the others had gone out. I was busy looking through the work they had done.

Anne was extremely small for her age; very pale, with features reminiscent of Egyptian paintings. This impression was intensified by the abundance of dense black curly hair, which she wore like an enormous wig, and even more by her stony calm expression.

I asked her why she was depressed.

'Because I am so alone,' she replied.

I asked her whether she had no friends among the girls.

'Not really. Everybody seems to me to come from a strange world,' she said, adding that none of her family had been found alive. She cried silently.

I asked her whether she would like to tell me more than just the dates of her past, and she told me the following.

Her father had been taken away first, followed by her mother and small brother in 1940, so that only she and her bigger brother were left in the ghetto. They were both sent to Auschwitz in the summer of 1943, and from there, together, to a mixed camp (a rare exception), where they both lived and worked until the start of 1945. For nearly four years, her brother had looked after her. She described how he had been like a father and mother to her. He had sheltered her. After they were separated, she had never seen him again. She had heard from people who were with him at the time that he had been killed a few days before liberation attempting to escape and reach her, when she was in a camp only a few miles away.

She cried when she finished and said, 'You cannot live alone. Human beings live for somebody else. Always it is so. It must be so. I lived for my brother and he for me. I cannot be interested in anything. I do not want to think about the future. I do not want to think about anything… I do not believe the present is real.'

I interrupted her at this point and asked what she meant.

'I walk along the street,' she said, 'and I see a woman coming towards me and I think this is my mother. I know that it cannot be her. But I cannot believe it. I cannot believe that I am here, and that everything is as it is.'

I tried to help her by telling her that, at her age, girls usually wanted to go away from their mother, to live without her, away from home, with other people, or by themselves; that she was at an age when to be without her mother would be a normal state of affairs.

'I know that what you say is true,' she replied. 'But I can't. I cannot live without my mother. I still need my mother as I much as I needed her at the time when I lost her.'

Here, I think, she touched on the crux of the matter. She felt she had not developed emotionally since the moment she lost her mother. She was not able to grow 'as her mother's child'. Reality gave her no chance to do so, and her pain and her fidelity forbade her to develop further, to attain the independence due to her age. Of course, she was just as independent and capable of looking after herself as any of the others in day-to-day life, but what she missed was six years of growing up emotionally. The development of the child of ten, who emotionally depends on her mother, to the young girl, who is half-turning away from her mother, and towards the world, free to look out for new emotional experiences—Anne did not have. Her attachment to her brother, who she said cared for her like both a father and a mother, who shared the following years with her, apparently did not fill this void. Perhaps he also had suffered from the same problem and had wanted to remain with those with whom they had lived at home.

After my talk with Anne it became clear to me that I had to know more about the girls in order to be able to understand them better. In other words, I needed to show a personal interest in each one.

I had thought that, as I had so far offered them nothing that was not connected with learning and knowledge, I had fulfilled my responsibility in sheltering them against disappointment which could have been caused by having me as an object for attachment. I knew I would in all probability not be with them long enough to see them both develop such a relationship and outgrow it. My decisions about my own future could not be dominated by their need, ready as I was at the moment to work for them. On top of this, and strengthening my resolution to be cautious, was the fact that the young people, such as those I had found in Windermere needing to replace the loss they had suffered, were looking around greedily and would form intense personal relationships very easily, and would therefore suffer another loss very severely. It was obvious that they had to be sheltered from this kind of disappointment. I felt acutely that I was an unsuitable object of their interest for all the aforementioned reasons.

The kind of teaching I had done was not just about transmitting facts. Teacher and pupils had also become aware of attitudes towards life and its problems. Through my approach, it seemed they had started to like and trust me, just as I had started to like them. Now we wanted to know more of each other. I also felt that they had a great need for something I could easily be—the teacher, aunt, distant relative, or older woman who is a very useful figure in young girls' lives. Somebody from whom to learn. They must have missed this sort of person very much in the camps where there were only young women together, with the only exception of SS women who, if they were not young themselves, were certainly were not a pattern to be copied.

I trusted that what we had built up together was sound and solid enough, so from that moment onwards, I risked showing my personal interest in them and accepted their confidences.

Re-enacting the past

At the beginning of May, The Jewish Theatre in the East End gave a performance to celebrate the anniversary of the liberation of all people in concentration camps in Germany. A short play was staged which had written for the purpose by a few of the boys and an experienced grown-up. It showed a sequence of scenes from the life of the children: the Gestapo taking them, scenes from camp life, and the liberation. All of us went to see it. It was met with great applause and many of the girls had tears in their eyes, but Susan criticized it afterwards and the others agreed with her.

'They are not talented,' she said. 'There is nobody among them who has a talent. It was not even one per cent of what it was. It was only scenes from our life. It was not more. It should have been more.'

She was in the rare position, with the others, of seeing her own experiences presented on stage and felt the play had not done justice to her expectations, or even to her memory. What had happened on the stage—her own intimate experiences— should have been lifted above a mere spectator's plane and needed to present a new aspect in order to satisfy her. It needed to be more.

I found this interesting, but like the rest of us was not in a position to confirm what she was saying, as my own experiences had never been reproduced with such accuracy on the stage. The girls, on the other hand, were seeing very dramatic events from their own lives acted out in detail in front of them and for them, and it had proved unsatisfactory. Why did they find it so? Was it that they resented that what happened on the stage was 'theatre' so had no real consequences, whereas this same thing in reality had proved so fatal for them? Or did they object to the suggestion that their dreadful experiences had remained for them exactly what they had been at the moment when they had happened—whereas in actuality they had used them and transformed them into something else? Was this enigmatic 'it should be more' perhaps purely aesthetic criticism, denying approval to something which was not a piece of art? I was in no position to tell. But I could not help thinking about how nine months earlier, when they had acted for us in Windermere for the first time, they had chosen comic scenes from Jewish life rather than the immediate past. This being so, I felt it was a good thing they had seen it acted out now, had cried while it was presented, even if afterwards they had turned it down, for whatever reason.

Everybody is bad

In our lessons about the structure of the molecule and the atom, I had tried to give them a conception of the strange repetition of patterns in both the universe and the atom. We spent much time talking about distances and proportions. I got the impression that this was of great importance to them and I thought of the similarity with the healing process of a bodily wound.

It looked to me as if what we were doing was helping them towards a greater elasticity of scar tissue.

My notes of that morning said: Listening more attentively, more friendly and interestedly than ever.

Towards the end of the period they wanted to know where the soul goes to when one dies.

Me: What do you call our souls?

Susan: Our thoughts.

Me: Yes, our thoughts and wishes and desires, our planning of the future, our knowledge of the past, our feelings of joy and pain, our fear. All this together.

Agreement around the table.

Me: Now let us talk first of what we think happens to our souls during our lifetime. Do they grow with us and develop, or not?

Ellen: No, all our lives we have the same souls as the one we were born with.

Susan: Oh no, a few years ago I wanted to do quite different things and I thought that the world was good.

Me: What is 'good'?

Susan: If a person does things to help somebody else. But nobody is good. We have seen it. The world is bad. Everybody is bad. Perhaps one in a thousand not. But the world is bad.

All agree. Very emphatic about it.

Susan: We were good before. I was good at home. I was a good child. Now I know how bad the world is. Now I know I am bad. Everybody is bad.

Me: Can you tell me once more, please, what you mean by good and what you mean by bad?

Susan: A person is good if she is friendly and helpful with somebody else who needs help. But nobody is good now. Everybody is bad.

Again, all shout their approval of this statement.

Me: What about the following people?

They interrupt me and shout: Everybody is bad.

But I insist that I personally know children who were hidden by people, and these people would have been killed if the children had been found in their houses, so I ask, 'What about those people?'

They, all talking at the same time, try to make it clear to me that these people did it at first because they were given a lot of money, but later, when the parents of the child were dead and when they therefore received no more money, they could not afford not to go on hiding the child, because if it had become known that they had done so, they would be killed themselves.

Me: Do you really think then that everybody is bad, and that there are no exceptions?

Miriam: One in a thousand perhaps is not bad. I knew an Aryan woman. She was with us in the camp. She was also a prisoner. She went into the camp because she was the servant of a Jewish family and she did not want to be separated. We all thought that she was good. But the world is bad.

With great insistency, passionate pathos, triumphant, and as a group compacted as a piece of marble, they all agreed that their world was bad.

Me: Anybody want to tell us some more about the badness of it all?

Susan: In the old days there was always persecution of Jews. And wars. Is that good? And in Poland everybody persecuted the Jews.

Me: You who have made these experiences, would you say, 'In Poland everybody is bad?'

Them, shouting: Yes, yes!

Susan: Nonsense. Being bad has nothing to do with a nation. All people are bad.

Me: Would you agree if I said, 'The Poles learn from childhood onwards to hate the Jews, therefore the Poles are bad?'

Them: Yes, yes, that is what it is.

Susan: No, the Poles are not bad because they hate the Jews. They are not worse than other people. It is the same everywhere.

Me: I think the Poles are always bad where they hate and persecute the Jews and often good in other ways.

Susan agrees - the others follow suit.

Me: The world apparently is good and bad. Your experiences prove that. Now it looks to you as if it were terribly bad, only ever bad, but Susan has said she was a good child. Well, she was part of this world when she was good, and perhaps she was also sometimes bad when she was a good child. Small children want the world to be always good. They cannot bear to see something wrong in it. If something goes wrong, they think they whole world has gone wrong.

Susan interrupts me: We are like that, but for us everything has gone wrong.

Me: Yes, and therefore you see the world as small children do and therefore you need help.

Anne: But who can help us?

Me: I think if you try to watch people, and do not expect of them to be good all the time, just accept them as they are, it might help. You would help yourselves. It seems we have gone away from what we wanted to talk about.

Susan: But that is part of it and is of great importance to us.

Me: Yes, but what about our souls?

They unanimously declare that they want to know what I think about the question: Where does the soul go to after we are dead?

And it looks as if I shall have to make a confession of my faith. I tell them that I think my soul must be very much tied up with my body and that when I die my soul will do a similar thing to my body, and dissolve into wherever it came from and what it was made of. That I do not know where that was or what that was, but I believe it must be something from which all souls came and were made, mine and all the others. Those who lived before us and those who live now and those who shall live in the future. That I thought all souls had something in common with each other. That I thought that with my death my soul, as I have it now, would stop existing, but not what it was made of. And that I know I could not know anything really about it, but that did not worry me now at all, though I remembered that there were times when it had.

Miriam: Do you know how it is with me? I believe in fate. When things happen, I think, well, this is fate. You cannot do anything against it. You just have to accept it. That is fate, I say to myself, if fate proves to be good for me. I have often seen people, many people, who have been trying so hard to avoid this, to avoid that, to be clever and who did this and did that, and I never tried at all. And here I am and am alive, and they are dead. It must be fate. And now—often I do not know what to think about Palestine and I get so frightened. I think it will be this or it will be that. Perhaps it will be good, perhaps it will not be good at all. But then I think: Well, this is fate. If it will not be good, I have to bear it, because after all I am weak and fate is strong, and fate works it out for me, and I cannot change it. I do not mean it is good and I do not mean it is bad. One does not know. Fate is stronger than I.

Susan: And I say—no. I cannot bear it that fate should be stronger than me. If only I want really hard enough, I can decide my own fate. That is what I think. Not that I can do it (with a smile towards me). I have a weak will. But I cannot bear the idea that fate dominates my life.

Ruth: Oh, you two! I know, because I have learnt it. I know that there is God and He is in heaven and He plans it all for me.

Rose (the oldest one among them, sister of Georgette, very natural, very motherly with her sister): What do you think about it, Mrs. Paneth?

And the others join with her. There are questions: What do you think about God, Mrs. Paneth? Is there a God?

Me: I think that all three girls have actually spoken about the same thing, about the power, or the law, or the order, which seems to be there and to be responsible for our being alive and living, as we are. Miriam calls it fate and feels it works it out for her. Susan does not want to think it is something outside of her, but a force inside her. And Ruth who calls it by the name we have all learned to call it by when we were children—God—sees it in her mind, where she had been taught to see it when she was small, at home and at school. I think all people feel that a human being is a small thing and have a longing for law and order and want to see an aim and a reason for life in this universe.

Ruth: But Susan said she thinks she can do it all without God.

Me: I do not think she said quite that. She said she cannot bear thinking that fate, something outside of her, could rule her life. I think she has had such experiences that she concludes from them that fate has been bad, and she cannot trust it. She feels frightened of what comes from outside and wants to feel that the good and wise inside her will be powerful enough to look well after her. We all need God as a protection. Where we see him or in what form, whether as a kind father, or not so personal, whether inside as our own instinct and will power, or outside as fate; always we want help and protection from it.

A few: What do you believe?

Me: I do believe that what happened is right. Not good, or bad, but right, because it had happened. That it has happened convinces me that it had to be so. I say yes to what happens. I think that everybody says yes somewhere.

They say nothing to this, which must sound strange and cruel to them. And the period is more than over.

Visit to the science museum

We had arranged to go to the Science Museum the next morning. The girls were very enthusiastic and once more said, 'This is the best we have ever seen.' We were given a demonstration of the theory of splitting the atom. This was done in a huge glass case, with a bombardment of ping-pong balls representing electrons. I was certain nobody understood any of it. Before we left, the girls bought themselves the inevitable picture postcards. The undisputed favourite was one showing a primitive half-naked man clothed only in an animal skin, carrying a lamb thrown over his shoulder while walking over a rough piece of country. He was No. 1 of a series showing the development of transport and was the only exhibit in the Science Museum containing a human being. Their next choice was the Wright Brothers' first aeroplane.

In the morning, we learnt about Buddhism.

Susan: All religions are the same at the bottom. Why can't people live like that?

Disturbance in the classroom

The mornings in our schoolroom were now very different to how they had been in March when we began. Had it not been for Ruth, the time we spent together would have appeared like a normal course-working period for eleven young people, they had calmed down so well. Ruth was the only one who still deliberately disturbed our lessons. At the beginning, she had been no worse than any of the others. Now she was a real nuisance, trying to divert attention by fooling around. She often succeeded in making the girls laugh, but I was unable to join in as she did it in Polish. Ruth was the one who had earlier said she had obeyed her mother, but since her mother was dead, she did not intend to obey anyone else. Her clowning around had become much more noticeable lately. She was not openly unfriendly or impolite towards me, but the others started to show they resented her behaviour. She had formed an intense friendship with Ellen, who often joined in with the rowdiness, though in a meek fashion.

This is how I attempted to cope with the situation. Although our group work was clearly important, in this particular situation it was Ruth who needed protection, not the others, so when the girls became disagreeable towards her because of her behaviour, I told them in front of Ruth that it would be better if they could manage not to mind, and that the disturbance, though disagreeable, had to be borne. Ruth must have had a reason to behave like this, and we should respect it and ease the situation by getting on with what we wanted to do, instead of becoming upset. I said similar things three different times on three different mornings. Ruth was always calmer for a short while afterwards, but then she would start up again.

Three days after our first 'religious' talk, the girls told me they had been arguing for hours and hours over an issue and would like me to help them solve their dispute.

What was it about?

The miracle of Hannah and the passage through the Red Sea. Ruth believed in it and the others had turned it down as impossible.

It seems that Ruth had now found an outlet for her aggression, which had been crystalized for her in this story. She believed in miracles, but the others did not. She was sure I would not either, so she blamed the other girls' views on my influence. I was glad I was called upon to help resolve their disagreement, though of course it was not Ruth, but one of the others who approached me. I forget which one.

Quoting from my notebook again.

Ruth: I believe in the miracle of the Hannah in the desert, and of the crossing of the Red Sea. God had worked it for the Jews. How could they have otherwise come across?

To my astonishment her friend Ellen was the leader of the opposition.

Ellen: How could it have happened? The sea cannot divide itself. It cannot be true.

Me: If Ruth believes that it happened as described in the Bible, then it is true for her. Why should it be so important to you Ellen, that it did not happen like that? It is such a long time ago that it happened anyhow.

Ellen: I do not want to believe anything that is not true.

Me: How can you know what really happened such a long time ago?

Susan and Ruth: What do you think, Mrs Paneth? Do you believe in the miracle of the Red Sea?

I was caught. There were no half-way measures for them.

Me: I think that it is impossible for us to know what happened six thousand years ago. Of course, extraordinary things are happening now. People tell about them, and in telling they become even more extraordinary. And if one sees the reasons for these extraordinary happenings linked up with events which one very much has hoped for—or has dreaded—and if one feels they are so extraordinary that no normal explanation will do, then one calls it a miracle and says God has worked it, or as the Greeks said, a God has done this for me or against me. I believe things, extraordinary things, do happen, and though I would very much like to know how they could have happened, I have given up thinking that I can explain them myself.

Ellen: The burning of the Jews now. I think that might be looked at by future generations also as a miracle.

Susan, very indignant: A miracle? But there is a difference. The Hannah and the passage of the

Red Sea were miracles wrought by God, and the Cremation was done by men.

Ellen: There is no difference. They will also say that God did it.

Anne, very shocked: Do you mean to say that Hitler was a God?

Great tumult.

Work goes on

This was an example of us talking about a theme not directly springing out of the material we were studying, but purely a problem they had brought forward themselves. I therefore concluded it was of real importance to them—or to be more specific, it was both of real importance to them to discuss the matter, and also to know where I stood on such things. During these weeks, a lot was happening to them, and it was as if they were taking stock and trying to find out what was still true for them. These eighteen-year-old girls were effectively going through an acute phase of early puberty.

Ellen had started to write a diary. The others were soon writing diaries too, without exception. Every morning when I arrived, I found half a dozen of them scribbling away like mad in exercise books, filling one after the other, or indulging in endless letters to some friend or other. Some of them carried on with their own writing even after I had started the lesson but would stop if the lesson interested them. I let this pass on the understanding that how they spent their time was their own affair. Some, like Rose, for example, felt this was impolite, and said so. This made an impression on the girls.

Ellen said, 'What I write here is of great importance to me.'

When I asked her what she was writing and told her that I would like to read it, but was unable to because I knew no Polish, Ellen said, 'I write what comes into my mind. If you could read, on each page of our diaries you would find that we want to die.'

It had become clear, in the meantime, that there was no chance of an early departure for any of the girls and that they would have to start training for a trade or profession in the autumn, or else start work. We talked about their wishes in this respect.

Susan complained that she could think of nothing that would interest her enough to take it up as a job. 'I do not know whether I am strong enough to build up a future for myself independently,' she said.

When I asked what was stopping her, she said, 'The day, at the end of my stay in the ghetto, when I was taken away and sent to Auschwitz. It is now much more present than before. I did not feel it then, as I feel it now. I cannot hope now. I cannot forget. There are a hundred small people inside me, and each wants something else. My diary tells about this.'

They all agreed with Susan that life was much harder to bear now. In the camps, they had had hopes, they said, but now they had no hopes anymore. They compared their lives with those of the people around them.

'We always see the other people now.'

Susan: We are not jealous. It is something else. It is everywhere the same. I shall have nowhere what I want to have.

Me: What is that exactly?

Susan: My home, with my mother.

Under the date of this conversation, I found a note in my diary saying: They behave much better, but apparently suffer more consciously. Only Ruth and Ellen still very childish in their behaviour.

This was their daily routine during those months. They made their beds after breakfast. Then lessons until lunch time. English lessons until four o'clock. Then they either did their washing, ironing, mending etc., or went out shopping, or for a walk, and to the cinema frequently in the evenings. Once a week they went to see the new programme at the Jewish Theatre. The gaps between these occupations, and many evenings, were filled with the above-mentioned writing, which became more and more of an obsession.

Our period of drawing and painting had developed into an activity which was very popular with them all - except for Ellen, who had stopped after her first two attempts. She was genuinely disgusted with what she had produced and my attempts at persuading her to go on had not been successful. She sat and read a book while the others painted. Lately, she had started writing in her diary instead. On the morning when we were talking about future jobs, she translated a poem from the Polish for me which she had copied into her diary from memory. This her translation.

When you shall live among foreign people
And things will go well for you, you will remember
Your house, your home, your parents.
The fear will overcome you
You might be lost among so many people
And with tears in your eyes you shall see
All this before you.

The house with the yard in front of it.
Such a poor little house, but so rich for you.
Inside four empty walls
And the white ceiling and the floor
And the chimney which leads to God.
That is so simple, so well known
As an evening in winter spent at the fireside.
And a mother bent over a cradle,
And in the cradle a child
And father looks on, slightly grumbling,
And the noise of the whole family.

Ellen admired this poem very much and said it expressed It so well. The other Polish girls joined in the praise.

They were now more aware of their own suffering, which led me to question the value of a process which brought even more acute suffering into the lives of these victims. I had not the slightest doubt that this newly developed ability to let themselves realise and therefore feel the full meaning of the old loss and the former injury was a positive thing for them. It meant they felt strong enough now to bear it, and also, they were ready to connect the early parts of their lives, the time of normality, with what they were living through now. It was as if they had reached back, wanting to reclaim the stump that was left after all the amputations, and although this was the region where the greatest pain was located and the touch still hurt them terribly, they were boldly attempting to fuse the two ends together; the new life with the old. This linking up would provide a continuity. Conscious suffering from their experiences was an inevitable step which they had to take. Soon they permitted themselves to slip even further back, as when Ellen remembered the poem. My diary for this date says, They talk a lot about their home now, telling me details about it. These memories, these talks about life at home, were astonishingly free from pain for them, and what they reproduced was simple, ordinary, friendly details of their childhood.

One evening, for some reason or another, the warden had forbidden them to go to the cinema. For the first time ever in their stay at the hostel, they obeyed this order and remained at home instead, painting pictures which were up on the mantelpiece for me to see in the morning when I arrived.

Palestine and Anti-Semitism

We were following the Crusaders on their way to Palestine and talked about their importance as carriers of strange cultures that had enriched Western Europe. The girls agreed they had learnt a lot by living in different circumstances in different countries; having to adapt themselves to and compare different customs. This was a happy time for all of us.

Miriam had received her permit to enter Palestine. When she heard the date for her departure was the following Monday, she went to bed feeling ill. She was very pale and restless and confessed to being frightened.

'I do not know what I shall find there.'

What she did find was an uncle with whom she did not get on well. First she went to a farming community but did not like it there, finding the life too hard and rigid. She left the community and went to live in a hostel where she trained as a nursery-school teacher. In a letter to her friend, she said life was hard, and she advised her friend to train for a job before emigrating to Palestine.

In a letter to me, she wrote:

Here isn't so bad, how I write always. Very often I write unhappy letters that is because I am in bad humour. I haven't a specially reason for it. Doesn't matter where and in which conditions— everywhere… I can't be happy. I suppose—you know what I mean for that.

Sometimes it is very difficult to write or even to speak everything what somebody would like to. The life is not so easy, and it doesn't go so how some people imagine it. It is not quite dependent on the person—it goes so and so, not often possible to change.

Anyhow I am not terribly unhappy, unsatisfied—but the whole reason is—I see everything in dark colours. I would like to change myself, but it is not easy. Maybe that soon will be better when I shall get used to everything, but it can't be good really.

She went on to tell me about her studies, and that her most urgent desire was to learn Hebrew properly. She ends the letter with:

… In two words can I tell you, that my feeling here is free. I feel that I am in Palestine only with Jews, that gives me satisfaction.

On the day Miriam left us, the girls wanted me to explain the existence of Anti-Semitism to them. I started by saying this was a complicated matter, but I would try to explain something about it. I asked them to give me instances of things that had made them or other people angry, willing to hurt, wishing evil—dogs chained up, starving, while other people had something to eat, etc. We agreed that people become aggressive when they were afraid. This could be because they were afraid another person might take something away from them, or hurt them, or infringe on their liberty, and so on. It might not always be clear what was frightening them, but it might simply be that something or someone looked dangerous, so they were not able to feel friendly towards it or them.

I went on to say something they all knew, that when the Jews left Palestine and went into exile, they had a law which ordered them to keep strictly to the way of life they had led in Palestine. They were not permitted to adopt the customs of their host-country, but had to live separated, keeping themselves to themselves, not mixing or intermarrying while they waited for the time when they could return to Palestine. In short, they were instructed to live as aliens.

Frightened people always turn against aliens, because the unknown is frightening to people who feel insecure. The man who lives next door but has never given you the chance to know him is frightening to a naturally fearful person, and suspicion will easily fall on that man if anything harmful happens in the neighbourhood. I went on to say that from the way the girls talked, I could understand why they thought Jews were the only persecuted people. This was not so, as they had learnt in our history lessons, but Jews had been picked on often, right up to the present day. Also, separating yourself from a community could never be interpreted as a friendly act, because it was not a friendly act. It meant, 'I do not want to have anything to do with you, for whatever reason this may be'. Therefore, this way of the Jews of keeping themselves to themselves meant that if people within a community got frightened, and aggression became rampant, the Jews were an easy target. This did not explain the savageness of Anti-Semitic action, but to my mind it explained the causes and the universality of it.

The girls listened gravely. There was no disagreement.

Visit to the National Gallery

Up till then, all the girls knew about art was anonymous, in much the same way as the treasures of the British Museum, though some of them had heard of Rembrandt. The moment had come to introduce them to the other great artists, so we visited the National Gallery.

We arrived soon after ten in the morning, when it was still empty. The girls investigated the works of the old masters as systematically as they had looked through the Natural History, Science and British Museums. They asked for explanations, wanting to know what each picture represented. Anne and Susan seemed most impressed. The others were also very interested. They studied every picture laboriously and intently, as only those who either have an unlimited amount of time at their disposal or are unaware of the number of masterpieces waiting to be enjoyed in the other rooms can be. They gave themselves to each picture, naïvely and unreservedly, taking their time. They also criticised. The shepherds should not be praying with folded hands, because that was not the way Jews prayed. Ruth could not understand why Christ was given different features by different painters. They compared Mary's beauty and found in some she was more beautiful, in others, less. They asked which one looked most like the real Mary. When they stood in front of one of Rembrandt's portraits, they were struck by something different about it.

'Why does this woman look as if she is still there, different from all the other people in the pictures?'

I suggested they go back and have another quick look at the Tintorettos and Titians, and the Bellini portrait in the first room, and compare the dates when those were painted with Rembrandt's dates. It was easy then, by linking with what they knew of history, to realise that Rembrandt's picture had been created in a later period, and that was why the style appeared new.

I grew tired and sat down on one of the seats in the middle of the room. The girls gave no sign of being ready to move on. I took the opportunity of watching them to see the impression they made on the other visitors. During the week, when we were in the classroom, it was always just them and me. Our visits to the museums and galleries gave me a chance to see them as an outsider would, and to compare them with other people.

There was no doubt they were conspicuous. Was it because they were so small and stocky? They were no taller than an average girl of twelve or thirteen, but their features were not those of girls, but young women. Or was it the eagerness that they emanated?

Susan approached me when I had been sitting quietly on my own for a while. She wanted to know whether people nowadays painted pictures, real pictures like the ones she was seeing here. I told them they did. The art of picture making had gone on in an unbroken chain for many centuries in many countries and was still going on now. Many pictures were now being painted every year, all over the world.

Straightaway, Susan wanted to see, them, wanted to know where they were, what they looked like. She had grasped that art is a genuinely readable and permanent medium by which people could express their culture and perhaps even more than that, and she was curious to find out and read the meaning of it all. I promised to take them soon to a modern art show, but Susan, right there and then, wanted a description of what those pictures looked like. I told them that life was very complicated now and had taken on many different forms, so artists were painting in many different styles. Some painted to show developments in knowledge of the universe and thought, some tried to express the importance of mechanical things and machinery in our century, others wanted to show the class struggle, and so on. Though there were thousands of pictures painted every year, there were only a very few really good ones.

'There is a man called Picasso,' I said. Many people thought his pictures would still be admired and kept in museums and galleries, just like those on the walls which they saw now, far into the future. He was a Spanish painter and was looked on by many as the greatest living artist. I wondered what they would say if they saw some of his paintings, because he did not mind painting impossible things—people with their eyes outside their heads, or with limbs resembling geometrical figures instead of human forms.

The girls laughed and wanted to know why he did this.

'Perhaps he wants to say that if you want to see yourself properly, you have to have one eye outside yourself, or perhaps he's saying that all the world looks at you, or you look out into the world with one eye, and at yourselves with the other. Who knows? I certainly do not. But his pictures are very beautiful, and they make you look and wonder.'

The girls listened intently. I felt it was possible that they, who only a few minutes earlier had asked whether pictures were painted in the twentieth century at all, could imagine Picasso conveying sense through his pictures. They apparently accepted my description of the sublime freedom from anatomical logic which he permitted himself as a legitimate manifestation of something worth expressing.

After this, they went back to look at whatever held the greatest fascination for each of them. They had split into twos and threes, and showed each other details, each group communicating with the others for this purpose. It was lovely to see them in this mood; full of an intense, pure and modest receptiveness, feeling the first miraculous imprint which great art can make on virgin soil.

The morning was over. We had seen what was in the first three rooms but had gone no further. We headed for the exit and bought postcards at the stall. A photo of the National Gallery building was their favourite, and they all bought one of these. While they were still choosing, a lady approached Anne. This lady had just bought a copy of the beautiful Details of Masterpieces from the National Gallery and wanted to give it to Anne. A highly embarrassed Anne refused the gift. The lady turned to me and explained that she was a Pole and had been watching the girls through the morning. She had listened to them talking, and as they were so very keen and it seemed to her obvious that they painted themselves, she wanted to give them some pleasure.

'One can do so very little, it is the least I can do, please accept this,' she said. I thanked her and took the volume.

Once out on the street her friends scolded Anne for having refused the gift of the book, but like a grand lady, she replied, 'How can I accept such a gift from a stranger?'

Faith

The question of faith and religion was still very much in the forefront of their minds. They discussed it often among themselves. In our lessons we had compared Mohammedan and Christian teachings, and they had stated they did not believe in anything anymore in a religious sense. This pronouncement, made by Susan and supported by the rest, was only opposed by Ruth who said, 'I believe.' The others laughed at her and told me she was not being sincere, because only yesterday she had made a sneering remark. Ruth furiously denied this. I tried to point out to them that most probably Ruth was in two minds about it. Everyone who had been brought up in a religious home, even if they came later to doubt those teachings, would still want to go on believing at times, and sometimes were quite sincere in their belief. Ruth was not insincere just because sometimes she seemed to believe in her old faith, and at other times doubted.

Ellen confirmed this, saying, 'I have faith because of the way my father described everything so beautifully. He explained, he described Moses seeing God in the burning bush so well I could see it. But now, having seen all that I have seen, I do not believe anymore. How can God let it happen that all the good people are destroyed and only the worst ones are left?'

I asked them whether they really thought that only the worst ones were saved.

Ellen: It is so. The worst ones were saved, only the worst ones.

Me: You want to say that you are the worst ones?

Them, in chorus: Yes.

Me: Why?

Ellen: My mother for instance. She could have saved herself; she was young and healthy. But she did not want to. She wanted to go with my little sister. And I live. Those who could not take a piece of bread out of the hands of somebody who was too weak to hold it did starve and could not keep alive. Who could not walk over the bodies of dead people, died. The worst ones survived.

I listened carefully, and it had struck me that in her description she had used the negative form. Those who could not... That gave me the courage to take the next step and cross the border of what distinguishes good from bad.

Me: There are many people, wise, good people, who think that it is most fundamentally good to stay alive, to have the strength and the will to stay alive. That that is Good.

Susan, interrupting: No, no, there are no ideas behind this. There are facts. We have seen it. The doctors, the teachers, the good people, who had learned something, the delicate ones, the noble ones, the better ones, were killed first. Hitler gave the orders that they should be killed first and they were killed first. People like us, who know nothing, who are not good, we live, we are left over.

I said I did not agree with them. I wanted to describe how I saw them, so I told them I was in a position to compare them with other young people because I had worked with many. The room went dead silent.

I said I found them truthful. They did not shirk issues. They were prepared to hear and understand the truth, even if it was painful, even if in the ordinary everyday affairs of life, they sometimes told lies. They had great discrimination and a sense for what was real and what people really meant. They were good and friendly and helpful to other people, and not hard, though they were very tough. They knew more of what it is all about than I had ever come across in other people of their age or even considerably older. They had experienced so much, and that had made them wiser. In trying to stay alive, they had been especially resourceful and adaptable, understanding and ready to take reality for what it was—grim though it might be. They had managed and learnt and grown through their experiences; they had not only suffered. They were capable of coming out at the end with qualities, which could only be understood by accepting the fact that ten or eleven years, as in their case, of living in good, happy families, with parents and brothers and sisters, where they learnt what was good and how people lived together, had made the good in them so strong, it could withstand all the evil of their experiences in the camps.

We had not expected it to be so. Before I had met them, I remember being prepared to meet young gangsters, young criminals. Now that we knew their quality, we credited their childhood, the things their parents had given them and taught them, for having kept them good, for having worked this miracle and enabled them to come out of the camps, ready to be good. They were not to worry about what happened in the camps. That had been a completely abnormal time. What they were now, and what they would be, was all that mattered.

'Yes,' they said.

We continued with our lesson.

It would cry

The girls told me they wanted to go to the theatre, to concerts, to hear and see beautiful but sad things.

'If I could play the violin, it would cry,' said Ellen.

They wanted to understand why they were so keen on tragic drama, but not at all on comedy, or funny, happy books. I tried to explain the function of poetic work, for both the poet and their readers.

Ruth told me she had written a poem on every new page of the notebook she used as a diary. I asked her to show me one. It was in Polish, but she translated it for me.

You smile at me,
Because now,
Empty and white as you still are,
As sheets
It is easy for you to smile.
Wait until
My writing shall make you dark.
How sad my writing makes everything look.

Then Ellen translated the poems from Polish which she had written while the others painted.

Auschwitz

I remember that day of Auschwitz
When everything was taken away from me
And one gave me rags.
With thousands of people
I was pushed into the barracks.
Is that all the protection we get?

Your bare walls without flooring
Sand only
There is no time to think.
Make yourself ready for appell.
They count our numbers and count our numbers
Without stopping.

When it gets dark
We are told to lie down on the bare earth,
Without food,
Without drink,
Without cover.
In the middle of the night.

Again, we are called for appell.
We stand until dawn,
Until dusk,
Until nightfall,
Aimless
And straight.

Dumb

Motionless
Silent,
Until at last after three days
Of hunger and exhaustion
We get food.

Everything hurts,
Limbs ache,
Feet hurt,
Eyelids shut from sleeplessness
Are those days spent in hell?
So slowly they pass.

And the eyes stare into heaven without hope.
They doubt that there is a God up there.
Because there is no pity anywhere.
It is cold
And we are filled with hunger.

One had to go on standing for whole days
And there is no ray of sun.
And people fall down and are dead,
Even before they go to the gas chamber.
And the fire of the sacrificed in the Crematorium
Rises high.

And it cries:
'Your soul I shall take as well.'
It calls.
I see death in front of me.
I look into the fire and laugh
And scorn at life.

Whether I have fever or am ill with disease
I stand barefoot in the yard
I do not feel the strokes of the rod on my back
It takes away all feeling
To be without pity,
And death laughs from over there.

The electrical wires move slightly
And it looks as if they were calling us.
A quick thought strikes us
To go towards them
And to touch them
The current would take away all suffering.

Oh, the weak willpower
The fear,
It holds us back from everything
Therefore, through all of our
Long lives
Our souls must suffer.

And when I almost lose my consciousness
The trains arrive and take us far away
Our hearts are still strong as steel
Therefore we must work
What for, and for whom and why?
Do not ask.

Factory

Sssssssss, there is such a noise made by the machine
That one cannot hear one's own voice
No air, one cannot breathe.
The machine is so big,
So terribly big,
And I feel so weak and small,
But I must work harder than the machine.

I do not lift my head.
I stand like that all day or all night.
I think a serf in medieval times has had a better life.
I may not say this loud.
I nearly choke from being quiet.
It is a terrible punishment,
To have to stand for twelve hours on end.

For which sin, which badness am I punished here?

When the day starts in the morning we are roused.
We carry our tired bodies to the factory
Every day anew.
Thoughts of freedom enter the head
And the gasses from the machine do their work.
They enter the lungs.
Small coughs spring up.

And every day which we survive is one day won
And a feat of courage.

Again, something happens to us.
Again, we are pushed into wagons
And again, we travel far in the cold
In hunger,
And again, there is a thought in our heads.
Perhaps this time we shall see freedom.
And we enter Theresienstadt.

We meet freedom.
And like a bird leaving its cage
We run out and into the world
To find home and mother.
Bad and bitter is this excursion
Because we find no home
And no mother.

Such years

Their diary writing went on frantically. They also developed a mania for doodling on tables, the blackboard, and slips of paper which they ended up tearing into tiny pieces, saying, 'We are so nervous.'

We had now had nearly three months of intensive work together, and had, as I have shown in my notes, discussed a number of topics. They had never at this point shown in their questions or answers a wish to discuss anything related to sex. Apart from the actual subject-teaching, they always took the lead in whatever we talked about. Sexual problems had not been touched upon.

The girls did not give the impression of having lost their virginity. They confessed to having committed many deeds which under normal circumstances would be punishable as crimes and which would have resulted in loss of life, but they had never given any clear hint that they had had sex with men. Perhaps they really never had, or at least not yet. I could understand, however, that they might look upon it as a crime in a class of its own, and unforgivable as nothing else could be. Was it harder to confess? And if so, why? Did they fear far-reaching consequences, so tried to wipe these out by denying the whole matter? Or was it rather that the loss of virginity under such circumstances was a small thing for them, who were neither prostitutes nor married women, but girls, who, when nearly dying from starvation, sold the only thing they had to sell, for a piece of bread, as one of the boys had put it. What they lost would have been a small matter compared to what they gained, so therefore were there two distinct values attached to sex for them? What happened in the camps was a different thing altogether from what would happen afterwards, and from what they had imagined it might be before anything had happened to them—what they had believed it to be in the eyes of everyone else.

In fact, only a very small percentage of them were going out with boys. Most of them seemed afraid of men and preferred the company of girls. There were cases of very intense homosexual friendships among them, between the boys as well as the girls.

When I spoke about the importance of their earliest years for their further development, I suggested we added a new subject to our curriculum—a combination of anatomy, physiology and hygiene—just enough to get a rough idea of how we grow and function. They were enthusiastic about it. I gave them a brief outline, with the help of an anatomy book, but I had hardly started when Ruth and Ellen began to giggle and to laugh coarsely at my descriptions and the pictures of the growth of the embryo. A few moments later, Ruth asked what venereal disease was, and how one got it. From the way she asked it, it was obvious she thought she was ill. We spent the next quarter of an hour finding the name for her ailment—the others also said they had the symptoms of fluor albus—and were reassured to learn that such symptoms were very common among girls and were due to malnutrition or lack of vitamins. It was easy for a doctor to distinguish this from a serious infection. The way the discussion had gone showed me they had all been worried about it to a certain degree, but Ruth was the one who had suffered most from the fear of being ill. She must have longed for reassurance on that subject.

From what the girls told me that morning, it also emerged that in Auschwitz and during their stay in other camps—that is, for years—they, along with the other girls and women prisoners, had not menstruated. Only one of them had had her period, and that, only once during her stay in camp. They had their own explanations for this and believed the Germans had given them a drug with their daily ration of soup which had made their periods stop. They did not want to accept the explanation that their bodies had refused to function normally under conditions which were so abnormal. For them, it was the drug in the soup. When I asked them why the Germans would have been so concerned as to give everyone a drug all the time, their answer was because it would have interfered with their work (an obviously fantasised reason) and because they had no rags, no towels, nothing. Menstruation started for most of them two or three months after liberation.

In my description of the ovum, they recognised a similarity in pattern with the universe and the atom. When I described the act of giving birth, I remembered how Miriam had some time ago told me she had witnessed the birth of four babies during her stay in the ghetto as they had been born in the room they shared with many other families. She attempted to describe her impressions.

'Such cries, such fears,' she said. She described how the baby was wrapped up in a blanket and put into a corner of the room and left there for two days until it was dead. 'What must it have been for the mother to hear her child cry all the time.'

Ellen did not want to have any children. She had been one of nine. 'I always wanted to have ten, now I do not want to have one. It is all too dreadful.'

When I asked her what was too dreadful, she said, 'It hurts too much.'

Everybody was very serious and interested, and though Ellen and Ruth pretended half the time to be studying an illustrated magazine, they were also listening intently. Ellen wanted to see the pictures of the anatomy of a man, which brought on a fit of hysterical laughter from Ruth, but on the whole Ruth had a better attitude towards us from then onwards. I could imagine an interpretation of her behaviour which would perhaps not be far wrong, and which she might have put into the following words to me, if she had been aware of what it was all about.

'You silly fool,' she might have said, 'talking and wasting our time with all that nonsense about stars and Egyptians and Romans and Crusades, when all that I can be interested in is whether or not I am ill with a most unpleasant disease that frightens me.'

When reassured, she became as friendly as the others, though I think she was less inclined to be intellectually guided by me, and much of what we talked about escaped her.

The second half of the morning was spent painting. Ruth painted a picture of a sailing boat with a man in it. There was a break in the mountain range, so you could sail through the gap, and a lovely pattern, into which she worked all the initials of the members of her family.

At the end of the morning Anne said, 'Mrs. Paneth, did you know that you had such artists here?' She was absolutely serious.

That same day, Charlotte painted a rainbow and said, 'I have not seen a rainbow for such a long time!'

Rose painted a train and said thoughtfully afterwards, 'I do not feel well since yesterday, because I got a letter from a cousin who is at home. Now I have painted the train. The train which took me away from home. People are queer.'

Gina, who painted the street said, 'Wherever you turn, it never is right.'

Lena painted a picture of a flowing river with low hills on the horizon over which the sun appeared.

We talked about the sense of security which a child gets from its mother. The atmosphere in the room had never been so good. In the course of the description of the development of the personality and the relationships within the family, they talked about their wish to be boys. They were emphatic about this, without exception.

Ruth gave this reason: 'They have to suffer less pain. Boys are not so bound up with a family. Sometimes the father is better than the mother.'

That same week, the girls specially requested we go to Madame Tussaud's Gallery to see the Famous and the Infamous. Henry the Eighth was their favourite exhibit, 'because he killed his six wives'. A few of them raised their fists and spat in front of Hitler's image, and others maintained emphatically that he had been 'much bigger than that'.

The tea party

One Sunday afternoon, at the beginning of June, I invited six of the girls to tea. They arrived half an hour late and were very natural and easy guests, interested in the pictures in my studio. They enjoyed the food, and conversation was lively and free. At that time, they did not know other people who lived in their own homes as all their friends lived in hostels. This home of mine initiated conversation about a possible future. Georgette was the first one who spoke of this. She had no doubt that in time she would become a doctor.

'I work at it and I have no other thought,' she said. She did not yet know that she was aiming too high as she was increasingly being forced to miss school because of severe headaches. The doctors who examined her could not find the cause, but she had to stop school the next winter and take a long break.

At our tea party, Gina told us, with her usual display of determination, that whatever her work turned out to be, she would have to live independently of other people. She wanted to travel, and said, 'We always shall think that somewhere else is what we long for. Of course, it never is.'

She had perhaps the most pronounced character among them all, and was the most stubborn one, but the lump of grumpiness inside her melted away if she had a chance of doing someone a good turn, only to form quickly again when she was left to herself. Miriam was her most intimate friend, a relationship which dated from their stay at the same camp. According to Miriam, Gina had saved her from starvation by keeping up a sham friendship with an SS guard through whom she could get food and an exemption for Miriam from being sent on transport. Gina was still very attached to her, but Miriam had switched her affections to Susan by the time she left, and for a while Gina suffered acutely from the loss, though later on she seemed to recover and take part in more activities.

One of my guests, Charlotte, was a delicate and restrained girl who had received very little education in Hungary, but she was interested and attentive, even if she did not actively take part in our work. She gave the impression of being very sensitive to criticism of any kind, aware of her handicaps, hiding behind a veneer of aloofness. She was very feminine and wanted to become a hairdresser—a profession she had started to learn in her hometown before she had to go to the camp. As we sat in my room having tea, Charlotte wanted to hear my idea of what her future would look like. I started painting a picture of her as a young hairdresser with light, capable hands. She would love to listen to her customers' chatter through the six and half hours of the day, which would be the most she would work. I was sure she would be convinced she could not work eight hours a day like ordinary people. Six and a half would be plenty for her. She would create the most lovely, wavy hairstyles for pretty women and would send the ugly ones to her assistant with a friendly smile. She would have a nice home with pretty things in it and on hot summer days in her shop she would switch the fan on and sit in front of it to cool herself with many sighs. She would think it lucky that her profession included such sensible arrangements as a fan. If, by the end of the day, she found she had not earned enough money, she would tell her little assistant that this was due to the sad fact that she had never had a chance of learning arithmetic properly.

This kind of nonsense amused the girls highly and everyone wanted their future told. This gave me the chance to do something I had been wanting to do for some time. I made up stories about them which showed their shortcomings and weaknesses, their 'faults', some of which were disagreeable, but I was able to make it clear to them that I liked them none the less for that.

Gina was the next to be told about her future.

'I shall come to Palestine one day and call on you in your tiny, tiny house — one in a row of tiny, tiny houses. You will invite me to come in and see you. I will recognise your house by the beautiful starched curtains in the windows. When I come in, everything will be so tidy and so clean, you will invite me for a meal and all through the meal, which will be very big and very good, you will tell me of how dreadfully slummy your neighbour Mrs. Smith is, and how Mr. Brown, your other neighbour, is no good because he drinks, and that there is no communal spirit in the whole street, and the children are depraved, but you, thank you very much, are all right. And while I am still sitting at your table, Mrs. Smith will knock at the door and ask whether you can come over in the evening and sit in and watch her little ones, because she wants to go out. A few minutes later, Mr. Brown will come in and leave his dog with you, because he has to go on a little errand where the animal would only be a nuisance, and by all this I can see you have not changed the tiniest little bit, and are still the same hard-mouthed, soft-hearted creature you are now.'

And so on, and so on.

But when it was Anne's turn to be told her future, I refused to do it. I said I could not. The girls, naturally, wanted to know why. I said it was because I did not know her well enough to see a picture of her future, and also there was something about Anne which made it more difficult. She had something of the artist in her, and as I was an artist myself, I was afraid I might interpret her less objectively than I should and would be biased towards what I felt was similar in both of us. I thought it was wiser therefore not to try.

Five minutes later Anne, who hardly ever spoke, started telling me the following long tale, which she narrated in the presence of the other five girls, directing her words only to me, unasked. Without interrupting herself or being interrupted, she gave this long and detailed account of her misery.

First, she said all she knew about her future was that she had to be independent. She could not visualise anything definite, but neither did she want to see anything definite. Then she said that she could not forget the past. She could not sleep at night. Every night, the Aussiedlung, the day when the family was dispersed, appeared to her. She wanted to forget it. She could not sleep for fear she would dream about it. Then she would, indeed, fall asleep and I dream about it.

'When we were liberated, the first day, oh, life was so beautiful. I thought I can live. Already a week later I knew I was alone. I knew life was no good. I cannot talk. I am quiet all day. I watch another girl, my age, in the hostel. She has no mother either, but she can laugh and be gay. Why can't I? What is wrong with me? I cannot understand it at all. I cannot understand how people can be like the Nazis.'

She went on to describe four separate horror scenes she had witnessed. She spoke with great emotion, very pale and breathless, and repeated that she could not understand it.

'If my mother had died from a disease it would be different.'

Then she stopped. I agreed with her. It could not be understood, that human beings should behave as the Nazis did. You could only conceive of such behaviour as a disease. A person must be mentally ill to perform such deeds. Educated people had to believe it was a kind of disease, a disease of the mind, a kind of madness. In the end, it killed the people who had it, after having killed so many others. Some died from typhus and some from the Nazi disease.

She repeated that it was all too dreadful and that she still lived with the idea that one day she might find her mother.

It was time for them to leave.

'Poor Mrs. Paneth,' said Rose. 'She had to listen to all our stories.'

All their stories? What did she mean by this? I had only listened to Anne's story, which I had heard once before, but in a different version. The first time had been a record of dates. This time had been a description of what she had experienced and suffered. None of the others had ever done that. At Windermere, it had been done differently.

I think Rose wanted to express her gratitude. Her innate politeness grasped the situation, and at the end of the visit, she had wanted to convey by this remark that she understood and appreciated my efforts. But in order to say 'Poor Mrs. Paneth,' she had had to distance herself to a certain degree from the suffering, the 'telling party', and become a listener—but it was still 'our stories', and always would be.

At Windermere, it had been 'we' a hundred per cent, and not an inch of distance had yet been perceptible between what had happened and what was being told. But when, this time, in reply to Rose's remark, I said I was glad to listen if I could help by doing so, and asked if they wanted the whole world to know what they had experienced, they said, 'Oh, it is no use trying, how could the world believe it. Because even we, who have undergone it, who have suffered it, who have seen it with our own eyes, cannot believe it anymore. Though we know it must have been like that!'

Anne did not join in these statements. She stayed quiet. Again, I thought, this a sign that much had happened that year which would lead towards their recovery.

When I asked them whether they would like to see the facts made public, they enthusiastically approved of the idea.

A mixed batch of lessons

One morning, Ruth and Ellen were absent. I was told they had gone to the Head Office to see if they could arrange for a transfer to a new hostel where they hoped to join some of their old friends, who had arrived separately in the meantime from Germany. The two girls had said nothing about this to the Warden but wanted to find out first if there was a chance they could go before announcing they intended to leave us. They foresaw difficulties and wanted to avoid those in case they were told they could not move.

As luck would have it, the Warden chose that morning to come into our classroom for the first and only time. She saw the two girls were missing and enquired after their whereabouts. I told her where they had gone. She wanted to know the reason and I, in the presence of all the other girls, told her that I did not know. After she had gone, I apologised to the girls. I told them I thought I had made a serious mistake in lying on their behalf. The girls disagreed with me, saying they had thought it a friendly act. They said that it would have been bad for Ruth and Ellen if the Warden had heard they had gone without her knowledge. But having taken me into their confidence, I disagreed and told them so. I said that even with the Warden angry, I could have explained why I thought it natural that the girls would want to go to the other hostel. I did not approve of their secrecy but thought it understandable. I should not have involved myself in their difficulties. There had been no reason for me to do so. I disapproved of lying. It had happened because at that moment I had not been myself but had acted as if I were one of them, afraid of the consequences of my deeds. This was muddled thinking and wrong and I had made a mistake. I lived in a world where lying was a bad policy, and I wished I had not done it.

'Anyway, now that it has happened, I wish you to understand what I think about it,' I said.

They understood my apology.

Our lesson carried on with no further discussion of the subject.

'Now, we have no history today,' I said, 'but Ways of Living. Do you mind?'

'I suppose it is all right. It makes me feel more at ease,' said Gina.

Susan changed that to, 'Not more at ease, but better.'

They were very friendly with each other. There was no strain in the relationship between the two nationalities, but they overdid the admiration for each other's achievements. I thought they were copying my way of admiring their paintings, so I made up my mind to become more critical, and I was, though I cannot remember a single instance which I could relate as proof of this statement. This did not relate to my attitude towards their paintings, but towards behaviour and achievements.

With respect to the painting, my notes at that time speak of a change in the singing which had always accompanied this activity. They had sung Hebrew, Polish and Hungarian songs from the start of every painting period at the top of their voices, seemingly unaware of what they were doing. It had happened every single time and struck me particularly because I had not met with it in any of the other many groups I had worked with under identical conditions. But now, their singing had been toned down. They hummed very quietly, hardly audibly, like people do when engaged on work that absorbs their attention.

The subject which I had defined as Some of what we know of the growth of the human being, had now arrived at a description of the stage of a three-year-old toddler. Ruth wanted to know why all children refused their food at that age.

Charlotte refuted this: Some children don't.

Ruth: My mother forced me, my father said, 'You leave her alone, she will eat later.

All agreed that fathers were very nice. Soon everybody was talking about nursery memories, happily, excitedly, normally. Ellen, the poet among them and a very intelligent girl, put her head on her arm, hid her face and said, 'How good it was to be four years old—how I remember! How I wish I were that age now!'

Then she and Ruth started cutting pieces of paper into tiny shreds, throwing it about the room and laughing and giggling. The others were not happy about this, but when I said, 'Don't you remember, Ellen said only a few minutes ago that she would like to be four years old still, let her have the pleasure now, I am sure it is good for her,' they accepted it.

At this point it also became clear to me that working with this group was providing opportunities I had not been aware of previously. The unrestrained and unhampered discussion of problems with a person you trust and to whom you can speak as freely as if you were one person with four eyes, opened up possibilities to the other members of the group and gave everybody's work greater depth and richness. Ellen's wish to step back into her childhood, and acting as such, had brought her release, allowing her to be that little girl for a few moments. The others must also have profited, because they not only watched her and me in this situation and by inference understood that if they had similar urges I would tolerate them as well, but also the similar urges, which they must have had anyway, had been released by Ellen's action. It looked as if profitable experiences could be shared as well as harmful ones. What we did together, every explanation we found, every act and reaction that resulted, helped them all, because the different viewpoints of the different contributions, along with the results, applied to more than one of them. For some individuals, this might even have had an augmented value.

Sometimes I had the impression we were engaged in a creative act because of the way these instances, which sprang from a moment's demands, fell into place as if they had been planned, as happens when a real work of art is being produced.

That week's outing took us to the Tate Gallery to see the promised show of modern art. It was an exhibition of living American artists which included many straightforward landscapes and still lifes, some abstracts, and some portraits. The girls were as interested as they had been in the old masters. I noted their comments in shorthand as they spoke.

Anne, the painter, spoke first: I'll be honest about it. I must say the older ones give more pleasure. They are done with so much more work and care. These say the truth, but they do not satisfy. Are there no pictures as beautiful as the old ones done now?

Susan: One can see the whole life in the old pictures. These here are superficial.

Anne again: The portraits have no expressions on their faces. They have an expression, but it says nothing, people must stand and sit, that is all. The old ones show something different, completely different. You see the whole person on the pictures here too, but something is missing.

In this way they struggled and tried to find the words to explain what had impressed both them, and more sophisticated critics before them.

In history, we had reached the Pre-Renaissance period. In his book, Mainwaring describes the mood in Europe at that time extensively and I was struck by the similarity with our classroom. The girls and I had lived intensively and at high speed in our lessons, all the way through the ages which preceded The Finding of the New World, and now we were ready to find it ourselves. The great struggle taking place within them was only now being directed towards a march into the future. I told them it ought to be relatively easy for them to imagine the mood of the people at that time because in many ways it must have resembled their own state of mind now—feeling free, getting to know what was going on, finding a new orientation, feeling keen and adventurous for thought and investigation. There were striking similarities. They did not protest this idea, though it was the first time I had spoken directly in this way. Slightly amused smiles went around the table at my words. I think they understood I had used a little ruse, but they let it pass. Perhaps they were ready to be convinced I was right.

Soon my optimism received further proof of being well founded. Once we set foot on the new continent, the girls shifted their interest from history to geography. They complained that they had no knowledge of the globe. Now they wanted to be able to orientate themselves in space, so they dug down and studied maps diligently, even testing their knowledge by asking each other questions to check what had been remembered. This was the first time they had dared to find out how much or how little their memories could hold, all of which made me think that they were more inclined to accept reality.

Georgette and Maria's school had closed for the summer holidays and they had brought in their first reports. They had not done too badly, but one point stood out in both reports—their striking unpunctuality. As they had now joined our group in the mornings, I took the opportunity to bring up this problem for everybody. All of them, without exception, had this same inability to be punctual. I asked whether they had an explanation, but they did not. Then I asked if they could think of any occasion for which they would be especially unpunctual. They could not. I asked if there was any occasion for which they would definitely be punctual. No answer. What if they were invited tomorrow morning to be presented in Buckingham Palace to the King to get a decoration for a special display of courage? Would they be punctual at eleven o'clock on the dot, or would they be late even then?

'Late!' came the unanimous cry.

'What would you not be late for? Is there anything you would not be late for?' I urged. Again, no answer, then after a moment's pause Maria spoke up.

'Well, if I knew that my brother would come to visit me, I would be on time at the station to meet him. I would be two hours early I am sure,' she said, and laughed.

'Oh, that is different!' said the others.

Important answers

In the last week before we broke up, I brought them a list of questions and asked for their help in finding practical answers. The questions had been compiled by a UNESCO official who had sent me a copy. They had been asked by teachers in a few of the formerly Nazi occupied countries who were encountering great difficulties in their work with the children and hoped for suggestions and help from UNESCO.

I thought the girls might have a large amount of empathy with the type of children and youths the teachers were worried about and might have useful suggestions to make. I told them so and asked for their co-operation. It also might do them good to see how their difficulties were shared by so many others that a body like UNESCO was concerned, and that they were regarded as a possible source of useful information and could help others.

I also presented the list of questions to a group of boys who lived in a sanatorium and whom I knew as well. They were the same age as the girls and had had the same experiences and were also being taught regularly, just like the girls. I was keen to compare the two sets of answers. Here I submit, for comparison, a few of the answers given by the two groups to a few of the questions. The questions and answers which are omitted concern themselves with practical problems which we had no way of answering.

Question A
Our children are restless, nervous, irritable. How can we overcome these characteristics?
Boys: Take them away from the place they were born, because everything would be worrying for them there. At a new place it is better. If we were at the same place it would remind us too much.
Girls: Give them plenty of food!

Question B
Some of our children resent and resist the authority of their parents, teachers and other adults. What can be done to develop respect for authority?
Boys: Introduce religion. What age are they? Try to give responsibility. Let them help with younger ones, then they will understand that authority is necessary.
Girls: Wait; do not impose authority.

Question C
Some of our older boys continue to steal, gamble, and indulge in immoral practices. How can we develop in them better standards?
Boys: Give them more work, keep them busy. Let them mix in a good community. Ask the children themselves why.
Girls: Change the place. This gives them a feeling of new life from one day to another. With us it stopped from one day to another.

Question D

Many of our children are intolerant and prejudiced, especially towards those of other racial backgrounds. How can we best develop in them tolerance and understanding?

Boys: Forbid the teaching in schools that the Jews have killed Christ, or that only the Jews are clean, etc. Teach that all are alike. Let them mix. Show that all religions are good.

Girls: We were like that. We saw then (when they lived together) that the Poles were just as we are, perhaps slightly better. Teach that all religions are equal, and that the consequence of intolerance is war. The Jews find the just man the best man, the Christians the loving man, the Mohammedans the faithful man, the Chinese the wise man; do not teach them the powerful man, because he will destroy everything. He is responsible for all the trouble.

Question E

Our children are hardened to the fact of death. How can we make them more sensitive to the facts of life and death?

Boys: Children who have lost their parents do not like their lives. Life must become good again. Give them good conditions, teaching, let boys and girls mix. That is the most important thing. One learns to feel again. To love.

Girls: It is like that with us.

Maria: When we heard that somebody suffered, or was dying, we cried, we felt it so much, it made us oh so miserable. Now I can laugh at it when I hear about such things.

Rose: I could not go over a churchyard before. I walk over it now. I like to go there now. By day and by night.

Miriam: When my parents were dead, and I was all by myself I thought I wanted to die. When the Gestapo came and I thought in Auschwitz that they would kill me, I was very much afraid. I did not want to die at all.

Anne: Why is it that we are so hardened now?

Question F

What are the most important subjects we can teach our children today?

Boys: Education, knowledge, culture, good example, psychology.

Girls: Knowledge, sport (which we had not taught them yet), play.

Rose: Example by the teacher, he must show in his own behaviour how to behave, he must like other people, he should make no difference between rich and poor... between the good and the bad neither.

Maria wanted drama to be acted with the children.

Question G

We have many orphans in our community and school. How can we help them?

Boys: Put them into hostels.

Girls: Put them into hostels. Hostels are much better than homes, because there are always possibilities for some things going well and being nice and not everything rotten as it can be in a home.

It was clear that the boys and girls recognised their own problems in the list of questions. The girls expressed this verbally more than once, though the boys did not. In comparing the two groups' answers, I felt there was no difference in the soundness of the advice given by each group. With the exception of Question D, where the girls reproduced in their own way some of the things we had worked on together which had apparently made an impression on them, there was no evidence that the teaching, whether by me, or the young Quaker teacher in the case of the boys, had affected their attitude towards fundamental issues. It was likely that most of the seven hundred would have given similar sensible advice, thanks to well-digested experience and a realistic outlook.

The only striking difference, I think, was found in the answers to Question E: 'Our children are hardened to the fact of death.' This was the only instance where the boys come close to a clear admission that they identified the contents of the question with their own suffering. They said they had learnt to feel again, and by this means were able to make a small hole in the cover that had hidden them. The girls said they were like that, but otherwise did not really answer the question. They were still at that stage, they still suffered from it, and they said so.

The boys recommended mixing the sexes. They lived in a mixed community at the Sanatorium and spoke from experience, which helped them to say this out loud. The girls had missed that experience and therefore had no answer as yet. But they had asked 'Why are we so hardened now?' which could be understood as asking, 'How can we become less hard?' I tried to talk this over with them. It became clear that they had forbidden themselves from using their sense of compassion when they had witnessed acts of great cruelty. They could not afford to imagine what the pain and loss felt like to the person who was undergoing it. They could not even feel it to its full extent when it happened to themselves as it would have been too hard to bear. I called this a safety measure which helped them survive and said it would pass with time. Once they felt stronger and more at home in life and more capable of enjoying things, they would also allow themselves again to imagine what suffering for other people meant, and to empathise with them.

I reminded them that only a few weeks ago they had told me they wanted only to see sad films etc. and I wondered if this was connected. Was it perhaps that they were glad to find they could be sorry for the heroine in a book, because they had a growing awareness that they wanted to be able to feel like other people, as they themselves had been able to do before the catastrophe? It is the task of poets and writers to evoke similar feelings in people. They have to be good at it, and then they are of help.

I have mentioned before how I thought their emotional impotence found comfort in group life. This conversation shed some more light on it. They were speaking of their repressed pain more plainly and boldly now in their writing and painting. It was at this time that The Sacrifice and The Train That Took Us Away were painted.

A Jewish face, a friendly face

Summer brought our group work to an end. Only five of the old group came back to London when the holidays were over to start training for jobs there. It was decided that I should see them one evening a week to keep up contact and to help them with whatever they needed. We read short stories. I gave them a little help with maths problems or talked on subjects that interested them. Their attendance at these evenings was very irregular. They went to the cinema, or to visit friends, or excused themselves with urgent letter writing or hair washing, but a few always came.

Dressmaking was the most popular of the occupations the girls had chosen. It was not so much that it appealed to them all, but more that with their scanty education and language difficulties there were not many openings for them in other jobs.

The five girls were tanned and healthy looking when they came back to town. They had left the summer camp a week before the holidays were over on the pretext that Charlotte had a sore throat and the others were needed to escort her back. They were fed up with camp life, though three days later they wanted to go back. Charlotte actually wanted to meet her boyfriend who was on leave in London and whom she had not seen for months. She was the only one in this group at this point who had a steady relationship with a young man. He was a social worker whom she had first met in Germany. Most of the girls were still too shy to make friends with boys.

Susan and Anne decided to stay on the farm for another year to train for work on the land before going out to Palestine. This is how Susan described her experiences on the farm on her first twenty-four hour leave in London.

'I thought it was dreadful in the beginning. But I said to myself: you must see if you like it. There are many unpleasant things there, but there were many unpleasant things at the hostel as well. You should not look at the unpleasant things. You should look at the good things. And it has worked. It is all right for me. I am so changed now, Mrs. Paneth, I am interested in people now. It is worthwhile. There are fifty people there. That is a lot. And there are many very clever ones among them. I like watching and listening.'

This sounds as if she was reproducing the advice I had given her, but I have searched my memory and looked through my notes, and I am sure I never said this, so it is Susan's genuine description of how she found her new surroundings. All I had done, and I had done this frequently, was to try to explain historical people and events. Through this medium I had attempted to stretch their power of understanding, to help them accept reality and the inevitable.

When I visited the two girls recently, Susan wanted to know whether I thought it was possible to go through everything they had gone through and still be good. To clarify this, she said, 'There are here nine boys from the camps whom I find very nice. Not only ordinary—but especially nice. Even nicer perhaps than the other boys here. How is that possible?'

I suggested that they were what she called 'good' because of the good homes in which they had grown up during their first nine or ten years. None of the subsequent bad experiences could spoil that. This showed that what you learnt in the first few years of life was so strong it could withstand all life's attempts to teach something else later. In their case, all the goodness and warmth, the order and friendliness, the shelter and protection, the general feeling that the world is good, which they had learnt when they were very small, had not been wiped out even by everything they had gone through.

'That is what we have learnt from you,' I said. 'That is why I shall call my description of what I have learnt, Rock the Cradle.'

Both she and Anne, who was there at the time, approved of the title and liked it. After a bit, Susan said she thought character was stronger than hunger, though she added, wistfully, 'Sometimes—not with everybody.'

When I asked for an explanation for what she called character in this context, she said, 'If I feel that I should do it; if I feel that it is right through the voice of my heart.' And surely the language with which a voice speaks, and the strength with which it can utter, had to have been learnt in the home. I think what Susan wanted me to confirm was this: 'May I have the hope that we, I am good? That I am not bad?' She had been one of the most vehement speakers, only four months ago, for the statement: everybody is bad.

Later on that day I asked whether she preferred one of the boys to the others and had made a real friend among them. She replied that her best friend was still Anne, but that she got on very well with all the boys. They were fun and good comrades.

'This is of great importance to me,' she added, 'because before I came here, I was afraid of boys. We had always thought in the camps that the boys must be even worse than we, because they had an even harder time in the camps. They were ruined more than we were, I think. Now it is so good to see that they are so nice. That they are not really ruined.' (She used the word 'spoiled'.)

I think she was not just describing the boys, but also herself.

On the same visit, both she and Anne told me they had experienced many good periods of time, and that life was quite enjoyable now. They could both imagine it getting better and better.

Ellen and Ruth had gone to another hostel where some old camp friends of theirs were staying. While she was there, Ellen started to write a novel in Polish with one of her old friends. It was the story of a Jewish girl—their story, though they did not want to admit this. They translated a fair amount of it into English for me.

The beginning shows a happy little girl at school. The main theme of the first chapters is the importance of education, the value of knowledge, with some examples of Russian competitive methods at school, until the day of the German invasion of Poland when the little girl and her whole family are sent to a ghetto. They told me that from then on it was easy to write her story because they knew it all so well. The story came alive at that point and was interesting to read. The highlight was a long letter, written as a poem by a young man to the heroine whom he loved, before he was taken away by the Gestapo. It was a real love letter. (Ellen had a girlfriend in the hostel and was not interested in boys.) The young man in her book found a Jewish guard, who, because of 'his friendly face, his Jewish face', he trusted with forwarding the letter secretly to the girl.

What a lovely detail. What an olive branch, I thought, when Ellen read that bit out to me. I remembered how one of the most serious hurts the girls still suffered was the distorted view they had of their own people's characteristics. One of the things I heard most frequently when the boys and girls talked about their grievances was their disappointment in their own kin. Many, many times, I heard the story of the Jewish guard who betrayed his fellow prisoners. In order to understand this, both in fairness to the guards, and in order to understand how this apparent betrayal must have felt to the Jews who suffered by it, you have to know more about the situation inside the ghettoes and camps. I will describe the system which the Nazis employed, and which produced that situation.

The administration of the ghettoes and camps was left to the Jewish inmates with the exception of the Kommandantur, who were SS men and women, and the highest official body in each location. There was a Jewish police force, a Jewish group leader called the Capo and a council consisting of Jews, headed by one man, who was responsible to the SS for what happened inside the camp. These heads of the councils naturally wielded considerable power for as long as it lasted. In a place like Theresienstadt, where there was an average of forty-thousand inmates to be looked after, the post of camp leader was very important. Many of the inhabitants' living conditions depended on him. His decisions as regards himself and his fellow prisoners were often a genuine matter of life and death, both to him and many others. What the Jewish officials could do in their prisoners' interest was always in direct opposition to whatever the gaolers, their superiors, wanted to see happen, the only exception being whatever led to increased hygiene and sanitary conditions inside the camp. If they succeeded in other matters, acting according to their conscience, they could be sure of a short term in office, ending with extermination if not worse. Every step not taken in that direction but taken in compliance with the orders of the men who held ultimate power, was wrought with evil for many people, and felt by the population of the ghettoes and camps as a direct betrayal by a brother. This was inflicting a hurt in a category of its own, with consequences far beyond the brutality of an SS man.

The inferiority complex of the young Jewish prisoners was nourished a thousand-fold by these circumstances. What they heard of German propaganda, expressed through the vilest vocabulary, became 'the truth' for these unhappy people because such evil, created and strengthened through manipulation, could be found in their midst.

The leaders of the Nazi party had asked their own people to perform feats of moral acrobatics. The Jews were called upon to perform just as difficult distortions of their own morality when they were asked, for example, to contribute names to the list of those who would be sent to the gas chambers. We, as humans, have not learnt to carry such responsibilities. In our world one death matters more than the hundreds of thousands who had to go to the gas chamber. Many of the leaders chose to die. Some took chances and tried to prolong their lives, to bear the burden and live in a distorted form, carrying the weight of skewed morality. It is not for us to sit in judgement, who are outsiders and have not been tested in this situation. Nor do we stand for The Law. But our young people were there. They knew these men and women and had suffered because of them. They hated and envied them. And they had killed some of them at the end of hostilities.

It was difficult to extract these facts from them. They did not easily talk about this aspect of their experiences and felt ashamed because of the inevitable identification which they practised. Though they did not explain the hows and whys, this experience was condoned and cloaked in the general statement: The Jews are bad. Their thoughts must have run like this: I am a Jew—I am bad, and be followed with: The good ones among us have died rather than become guilty. I am alive, I am guilty. There were caught up in this dangerous cycle.

A young Polish girl of eighteen, an old friend of mine from Windermere (not one of my eleven pupils) told me that one day in May 1946, a year after liberation, while we were taking a walk, an incident occurred which illustrated what I have just described. She had been talking about why she thought the boys had had a harder life than the girls. They had been exposed to more cruelty and crime, but the girls' life had been hard as well, with too much hard work and too much hunger—but at the same time, they had felt sheltered, she said, alluding to the period after liberation when they had lost that shelter and felt exposed. Inside the four walls of the concentration camp, they had felt they had a home of sorts to return to when they came back from work. There was great comradeship. Everything was shared.

'The SS women were often quite nice to us. Some, I think, had pity. They gave us small bits of extra food sometimes. But the woman in charge was a bad one. She was still young and very good looking and elegant, but oh so hard and cruel!'

She went on to describe a scene from her time in Auschwitz.

'We had arrived in Auschwitz two days earlier and had already been separated from the rest of our families. We had been standing for two days and two nights in the yards, when at last we were led into a room where we were allowed to lie down on the floor. It was a stone floor and there were too many of us for all to be able to lie down at the same time, so we lay in rows, one half on top of the next, to save space. That way everybody could at least partially lie down, and nobody needed to stand. At first, that was all right, but during the night, the weight of each became a burden to the one underneath, and once in a while, one woman could not bear it anymore and tried to shift her position. This was not easy, as there was a tremendous weight to be shifted. While trying to do this, she woke up her neighbours. Her feet were cramping so badly, she let out a scream. After a few minutes, there was a general shouting and screaming. Hardly anybody knew why or how, but everybody joined in. We sometimes suffered from such outbreaks of mass crying or fighting, but this time, in the middle of the tumult, the Jewish Capova, the guard, appeared and made us stop, saying, "You should be ashamed of yourselves. Look out there, through the window. You can still see the glow of the fires by which your families are burning, and you here make such a noise. You really should be ashamed of yourselves." That is what she said to us! Can you believe that?'

This description, which is not something out of Grimm's Fairy Tales, but which happened in Auschwitz in Summer 1943, rings with madness. The childish warning of the angry person, who, distracted in her delirium, said You should be ashamed of yourselves. Whom was she actually addressing? The girls? Or herself?

Six months later, when I was writing up this event, I phoned the girl who had told me about it to verify the facts, so that there was no possible mistake that this had been said by a Jewish person and not an SS woman. She gave me the same report. But when she had finished relating the facts, she said, 'These people were the dregs. You must understand they were the leftovers from hundreds of thousands. Perhaps they were in the gas chambers once themselves and had come out alive. That happened sometimes. Or something of that sort. Or they were ill. It was quite abnormal there.'

I had not interrupted her. This was her own comment. She was ready to understand now, for her own sake—and for the sake of objectivity. What a step towards recovery that meant! Because it was that sort of experience, much more than the fact that they were orphans, that imperilled their future development. The purpose of rehabilitation was to enable them to look at their own reflection in the mirror with friendly eyes. Some of them were now well on the way.

Of course, there were ups and downs and setbacks. Susan, who only a few weeks previously had announced her intention to start living on her own when her year's training had finished, was in London and doubting if she would ever be able to summon up the courage to live independently, away from the group. Lena and Georgette were suffering from severe headaches and all sorts of other ailments and did not look well. Every single one of them needed more help than we could give them. This was a critical year for them. A steady flow of light and food, both mental and emotional, was needed to feed the young shoots so that they could grow into the solid wood which could build a future home. Our young people were in a delicate state and ours was delicate work.

Though we were often discontented and doubtful about our efforts and results, of one thing I was certain. The boys and girls had, during this period, sobered. The gush of hatred which had run through them had ebbed, because the bed in which the stream of their lives flowed had now widened. Fertile land had appeared.

Marie Paneth teaching some of the children in the Lake District

1/Ⅴ-46 y.

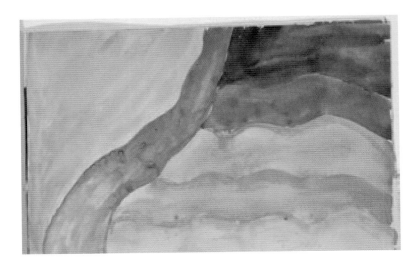

The following three photographs show some of the survivor children, who Marie Paneth was to welcome to Calgarth Estate, in the centre of Prague and were actually taken en route to the Lake District. At this moment they were being captured for posterity in front of the Jan Hus Memorial in the Old Town Square, before shortly afterwards being taken to Prague airport.

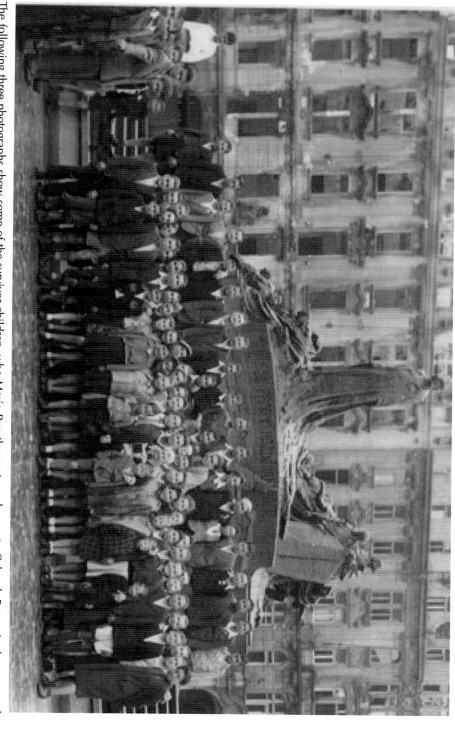

This colour photograph was taken in May 2019, commemorating the children's original departure from Prague to England. It includes some of those original children as well as many of their Second and Third Generation relatives. It was a truly momentous journey and occasion.

Part 3

The Struggle

I have spoken about the survivors. I have tried to peel out of the mass of superficial wrappings the truest form of this type.

A few among the seven hundred who came over to England could not be counted among them. Three died in the first year, two from accidents, one from tuberculosis. I knew the latter one slightly. He was quiet and resigned. There was no apparent struggle. He died ten months after his arrival here, after much patient suffering.

One more, whose name is Morris, is very ill with tuberculosis. I have visited him frequently over the past six months, so know him better than the other boys and girls. He is struggling desperately to find a balance in favour of survival, though he thought from the start that he would not live.

'I am a bitter person, that is why I am so ill. Bitterness means rot. Bitterness prevents from healing. A bitter person cannot get better.'

These were the words he used when he talked about himself a year ago, clearly describing his state.

For those who are interested in some details about this sad figure, I have included in this publication a transcript of the notes I made recording my visits to him.

Morris, age seventeen. Taken to hospital a few days after his arrival at Windermere, suffering from T.B. Very bossy, loud, cynical, very good looking.

His past history, as told to me twice by him.

Father, tailor, with a workshop at home. Mother, strict, had difficulties with Morris. He was naughty and rude, fought with his big brother who was three years older. There was also a seven-year-old sister and a five-year-old younger brother, who was 'very sweet'.

Morris attended the local Polish elementary school in the morning and the Jewish school in the afternoon. Mother tongue, Yiddish. Home, Orthodox. His friends said he knew Hebrew exceptionally well.

At the outbreak of war, he was eleven years old, big for his age and very strong. He was engaged by the Germans to work for them but still lived at home. His older brother was sent to a factory in the neighbourhood.

In spring 1940, the Jewish population of his small hometown in Galicia was rounded up in the marketplace by the Gestapo. Two hundred and fifty people with labour tickets, Morris and his father included, were picked out and told to stand to one side, while the rest of the Jewish population, men, women and children, were marched out of the town and shot in a nearby wood. The two hundred and fifty heard the shots.

When this was over, they were ordered to march to another locality in the neighbourhood to work at a factory. When they arrived at their destination it was found that due to some muddle they were not yet needed. They were therefore dismissed on parole, to return to work at the same place a week later. Father and son returned home in the meantime. It was a Friday, just before the beginning of Sabbath. The beginning of Sabbath is a time of great religious importance. The whole family assembles to take a meal together, which is accompanied by singing, the telling of holy stories and the practice of ritual. The mother of the house consecrates the meal by saying grace over it. This is the only time a woman takes an active role in any of the religious rituals of Jewish life, but this one is of great importance. Without it, Sabbath is not properly observed.

Morris's sister returned to the town and her home that Friday evening. She had been away on the day of the slaughter and therefore escaped it. His mother and little brother were missing. His sister said grace.

When Morris reached this part of his story he stopped talking, blushed and fought back tears. After a while he wanted to resume his tale but could not remember where he had stopped. I am reporting this in detail because it was not only very striking when it happened for the first time— he seemed to have been far away—but the second time, a few months later, when it happened again. Again, he broke down when he came to this first Sabbath without his mother, again he lost the thread of his tale, again after pulling himself together he asked me: 'Where was I?' and wanted me to help him to go on. It struck me as this was the point where he always wanted my help. The rest he could manage alone. This, he wanted to forget. Because of this he forgot the rest.

When the week had passed, he and his father went back to the factory and concentration camp. His sister stayed at home. Two months later she was sent to Auschwitz where she was gassed. His older brother was shot in a camp, weak from exhaustion. Morris and his father stayed together and worked in different camps in Galicia. After a few months, his father managed to obtain some papers by bribery. He had managed to take some money into the camp.

Here I interrupted his tale to ask if his father had tried to get papers for Morris as well.

'They cost a lot of money,' was his reply.

Then I asked him whether it was very sad for him when he found that his father could not buy papers for him as well. I had to repeat this question twice. He did not seem to understand what I meant. It was as if it had never entered his head that this could have been done for him.

His father succeeded in leaving the camp and got as far as Cracow. There he was discovered and killed. An eyewitness told Morris about it a year later.

Morris went through many camps. He had to work on roads, in quarries, on building sites and at the loading and unloading of trucks and railway vans. It was hard labour, under starvation conditions. According to his descriptions he did not spare himself. He liked to show off his strength and his toughness. 'I have learnt to work under the Germans,' he said.

By the end of March 1945, he was in Buchenwald. He was full of praise for the administration there. According to him it was a very clean place, where a premium was paid on any louse, in the form of an extra soup-ration. It was odd to hear one camp praised and graded against others, after five and a half years of concentration camp standards.

'We got clothes at Buchenwald. I always managed to look smart.'

When rumours spread that the Allies were approaching Buchenwald, the elders of the camp and the group leaders were killed. They were denounced as 'bad'. He agreed to these measures. Then everybody was put into prisoners' clothes. It was still very cold at that time of the year.

Morris had frozen feet which became infected. He had not been to work and had hidden in the camp. He knew what that entailed, but he had risked it. When in his hide-out he heard that as the allied armies were approaching the camp was going to be evacuated, he knew that to remain behind meant to be burnt with the camp, as had happened with a small camp in the neighbourhood. Therefore, when roll call came, he pulled himself together and marched with the rest of the men in front of the SS who inspected them.

'I walked, and did not even limp. I felt no pain in my foot anymore. I made the march with the rest of the others and my feet did not hinder me.'

They were on the road for eighteen days, under guard, without provisions. They marched during the day and slept in barns or in the open at night. The guards tried to get them food from the farms, which amounted to two potatoes a man at night if they were lucky. They started to eat grass at the roadside. There was very little of it because it was March. The guards hurried them on with their rifles. Anyone who could not keep up the pace was shot. Every night many died from exhaustion. Once he got hold of a raw turnip.

'I thought it was heaven.'

Confusion grew among the guards along the way. Rumours about the whereabouts of Allied troops worried the transport leaders. Morris described vividly how you could sense the SS men getting frightened—the change from hope to despair and back to hope among the prisoners, and whether they were preparing to revolt, to kill the guards in the night. New SS troops joined them a few hours before they would have freed themselves, and they were split up into smaller groups.

They arrived at Theresienstadt.

'There were girls there. They took us in. They washed us. Women washed us. We thought we were in heaven.'

They were given food, but they were not well enough to walk about as they were ill with typhus.

When Morris recovered, he went back to Poland where he learned the facts about his sister and brother. In the months that followed he travelled a lot through Europe.

He had told his story for the first time when he was recovering from severe haemoptysis. From then on, he had to stay in bed. His mood deteriorated badly. He became aggressive and paranoid. He managed to throw the whole ward into fear and confusion by his behaviour and gave the impression of being a terrified animal, turning to attack. He bristled with an exaggerated wakefulness. His hearing was over-sharp. He saw and observed the slightest movement and the smallest change in his surroundings and interpreted everything as enemy action. He was full of distrust and fear. He lined people up as if he had a plan for battle, dividing them into friends and enemies, weighing their importance, trying to direct them, chasing them about, testing their resistance to his moves, and creating a stir among the boys and staff. Helpless, at the centre of the whirlpool in which his enormous aggression was the moving force, he was wearing down his own and everybody else's energies.

I would sit in his little room by his bed when I visited him on the ward. There were days when he hardly talked, but fixed me with his gaze, watching for the slightest movement. On other occasions he asked many questions which expressed his distrust. He seemed to be convinced that everything had a hidden and harmful purpose, which we kept secret from him, and only if he could get hold of the right detail, which would betray us, could he bring this to the light.

He developed fantasies about the doctor, whom he accused of wanting to poison him, and about the young nurses, insinuating that they made sexual advances. He was determined to make one of them leave and threatened that 'there would be blood'. He accused her of being the cause of his spitting blood. He became quite unreasonable in his demands towards his friends as well. They were forbidden to touch any of the hundreds of roses with which a bush in front of his window was covered.

'If it happens, I shall tear the bush out by its roots,' he threatened.

Everybody was frightened, so he was sent to a mental hospital. He stayed there for ten days and returned to the Sanatorium much calmer. The mental hospital had made a great impression upon him. He talked about it. The variety of patients! He described what he had seen in detail and I was much impressed by his powers of observation. He had watched the male nurses communicating with some of the deaf-and-dumb patients on the ward. One evening, one of the nurses had, at Morris's request, shown him the deaf-and-dumb alphabet. The next morning, he had been able to talk to these patients through their own medium of communication. This had gratified him very much and had astonished the nurses. I was a bit doubtful as to the truthfulness of this tale, as by chance I had learned the deaf-and-dumb language myself and knew it is not easy to remember the signs. I asked him whether he still was capable of reproducing some of the letters.

'Of course,' he said, and he gave me the whole alphabet without making a single mistake, hesitating only twice to remember the correct sign. This is one of the instances when I learned to admire the make-up of his intelligence.

The teacher in the Sanatorium, who gave lessons to all the boys and girls there but rarely had a period with Morris as he was too ill to work, told me the following story. One day, he had tried to explain to his pupils the fact that the future has no reality, that only the present and the past can be credited with this quality. He had found it too difficult a concept to put across.

Morris, who had not been present when the others were struggling with this intricate problem, and to whom the teacher had told in two sentences what they had grappled with that morning, immediately produced an example which showed he understood the entire implication of the statement.

'That is like in our town,' he said, 'where there is an inn. The innkeeper put up a board outside, saying fresh beer tomorrow. People came in and thought because they had read the sign yesterday it might be tomorrow. But it never is, and the host is never under the obligation to serve fresh beer.'

The clarity of his insight often astonished me. He was capable of describing his own mental state and giving directions as to how he should be handled, as in, for example: 'Why do they argue with me when I am in that state? They should know that I am not reasonable then. They should turn round in the door, should say he is mad and leave me, and not try to talk sense,' or, 'I am the greatest enemy of myself,' or, 'I have lost everything, my father, my home.' After a pause he would add: 'I have lost myself too. Where am I? I am no more there,' or, 'My anger tears me literally. It makes a hole in my inside.'

From the time he was seriously ill onwards I saw a lot of him and soon we were having long talks with each other. He liked to discuss his disease, asking for many details about it, and he discussed the other boys. More than anything else, he liked to talk about himself. He often did that in an indirect form, as for instance when he asked me, 'Do you know what the two most important things in life are?'

Me: What are they?

Him: Health is number one. Do you know what is number two?

Me: No. What is it?

Him: Mother. (Said in a whisper, and in English, though otherwise we always talked German with each other.)

After a pause he corrected himself. 'No, it is not number two. It is number one. If you have a mother, you can easily be ill. It would not matter. What would it matter?' After another short pause, 'No, it is all wrong. It is not true what I tell you, Mrs. Paneth. Mother is not number one, she is everything. Nothing else matters.'

We had this conversation a month after he had been suffering with haemoptysis. One day I found a picture of a woman with a baby in her arms, cut out of an advertisement, pinned on his wall.

He told me once about a conversation he had had with the three boys with whom he had spent the first four months in the North in another Sanatorium.

'We had made up our minds that the whole world should be destroyed,' he said. 'And we made a resolution, which each of us had to sign; it was: We want the whole world to end. But only three of us signed. Sammy did not. He said he wanted to marry first. One of us is already dead.'

He nodded thoughtfully after a pause.

In September he was transferred to a private nursing home. He was very lonely there, all by himself in a room. I went to see him almost every day. In the beginning, he liked the food and the comfort, but he missed his companions, and soon became very restless again. A wireless and a gramophone were installed in his room and played music all day long. He developed an extremely strong passion for music and was enraptured by the works of Mozart, Beethoven, Brahms. He wangled gifts of records out of his visitors and got quite a collection together. But he became enslaved to the wireless and gramophone and could not bear it if there was no sound coming from either. He had the wireless on non-stop, even if there was no music being played which he liked. After a while, the administration of the nursing home objected to this incessant noise coming from his room, and he had to keep to only a few hours each day. This brought him to a state of despair mixed with rage towards the matron whom he held responsible for this 'cruelty'. He became rude and aggressive with the staff and thought that he was being very badly treated.

One of his worst grievances at this period was that the nurses sometimes brought him water when he asked for milk. He was not at all willing to accept the explanation that milk was rationed and that he got more than his share anyhow. The matron, on the other hand, complained that although he had detested milk when he arrived and would not drink a drop of it, now he could not get enough. She found this unreasonable.

'Now he complains to me in the bitterest tones about this and speaks about it as if it were the gravest insult,' she said.

He was very docile with me at that time, but inclined to cry at the slightest provocation, sometimes without any obvious reason. He had become soft and touchy, very much in contrast to the defiant attitude which he had shown previously, when his mood had seemed so taut and brittle it had been like striking a cord and hearing the string vibrate when anything touched him.

My diary shows almost daily entries about him from that time. I found him ready to speak and very eager to listen.

October 15th

He broke the fresh rolls which I was bringing him (daily) into tiny bits before he put them into his mouth. All at once he smiled at me and said, 'My mother used to break her bread into small crumbs and she held it even in this way,' showing me how she held it. It struck me that this was the first time that he had used the word mother freely and simply.

October 17th

Morris very upset and made a great fuss about his grievances. He 'cannot wait'. He 'gets water instead of milk'. He 'cannot have his music when he likes.' He 'cannot stay in the nursing home because he hates the matron too much.'

I asked him whether he knew what he reminded me of. 'You remind me of a silly mother who spoils her child terribly, because she cannot bear to hear it cry.'

Here he interrupted me with, 'Oh, how wrong you are. You think I am too fond of myself. The contrary is true.'

Then I explained to him that I had not meant that. What I really meant was that a mother who gives in every time she hears her child cry does not think whether it is good for the child, or not, to give in. She has no thought about the welfare of the child in her mind. She really only gives in because she cannot bear the crying, because it hurts her. It looks as if she is showing every consideration for the poor child, but really it is nothing of the kind. She is concerned about her own little suffering and the baby gets no help from her in its difficulties and education.

'That is the same as what you are doing with your inward self,' I said. 'You do not investigate whether this or that difficulty brings you some reward. You cannot bear to see yourself suffering by having to wait, for instance, or by getting a substitute instead of what you wanted. In that way you do not help yourself, but spoil yourself.'

'I know. I am an enemy of myself. I hate myself.' After a while he added, 'I think it is of the utmost importance for me to understand this. Do you think that one can still change at my age?'

October 18th

When I got up to leave, he said, 'Do you know Mrs. Paneth that you resemble my mother very much. You look actually look exactly like her. My mother was also as tall as you—perhaps not quite, but nearly.'

He was very upset and difficult. The nursing home had given him notice to leave because of his rude behaviour. He rang up the main office, made a few statements which were incorrect and was very unreasonable when I saw him.

October 20th

Told me about his lying yesterday. Calm, sensible and looks much better.

October 21st

Though he had refused to be moved and had threatened passive resistance, he went very calmly and apparently willingly with me to the L.C.C. hospital where we had found a bed for him and where he stayed for over a year.

He was in a big ward with two dozen other people, mostly old men. He was very lucky with his neighbours, one of whom was young and the other an especially nice middle-aged man who had a good sense of humour, understood and put up with Morris's moods and had a fatherly attitude towards him. Morris liked the ward. There was always something going on and he was not left to brood on his own. The steady friendliness of the male nurses was a special blessing. He still suffered from depression and bad moods once in a while, but was reasonable even while those lasted.

At the start of his illness he had worried a lot about his health. He observed, commented on, and worried about his temperature and coughs all the time. He had stopped that. During that first week at the hospital, he said, 'If I go on having these temperatures, there will soon be no Morris left to have them.'

There was a short period when he suffered from the delusion that his affairs were being handled secretly by a secretive power which was lazy and did not take his troubles seriously. This was directed against me. I think he soon realised I did all I could, but what I could do was very limited.

Soon afterwards, when I visited him, he told me that he had cried. I could see this was true. When I asked him why, he said at first that he did not want to tell me. A few minutes later he said he had had an extraordinary dream.

'I was being persecuted by the Germans. I ran away from them. Then I woke up. My neighbours said I had screamed in my dream.'

I expressed my compassion at him having had that nightmare.

He went on to tell me about another dream he had had that same night.

'I also dreamed of my parents. I saw my mother standing at the window in our street. She looked out and saw me passing by. She looked at me and followed me with her eyes. That means something but nobody can know what it means.'

I told him that I thought that it most probably meant quite a few things. He wanted to know what I thought.

'Perhaps it meant you long for your mother very much.'

He made me repeat that sentence and then started crying. We did not talk about it anymore. I think he was understanding the dream as an invitation by his mother to join her in death. That 'the waiting for him to come,' was an expression of his thoughts about the possibility of him dying soon, but he did not seem to be ready to express it any more clearly.

He also told me that he had broken three of his precious gramophone records that morning. That his craving for music was much less now. He was played it less than he was permitted, now that he was allowed to play as much he liked. The ward did not mind his making 'noise'.

His behaviour as an addict was gone.

Later in the afternoon he wanted to know how I spent my day. This was the first time in all these months he had shown he credited me with an existence apart from the function I had for him.

I told him about a meeting I was intending to go to in the evening where the problems we came across in our work would be discussed. He wanted to hear more about this. I gave him a few examples, such as what to do with boys who were untidy and unclean. He was very astonished to hear that there were any, and actually, there were very few among them. He wanted to know what was said in reply to this question. I told him that we all found that those were the boys who had other problems as well. They were not settling well into their jobs. They were either lazy, or rowdy, or both, etc.

'They seem to be angry with the world,' I said.

He nodded emphatically at this, saying, 'And one cannot do anything about it. It is of course no use telling them to be tidy.'

I agreed, and said, 'But perhaps one can help them to become a bit less angry. We all know that you all have reasons to be angry. The world has been extremely bad towards you, but still, only a few are as angry as that.' 'If we had not been so very young it would not have been so hard. But we were too young. If we had been older, I think perhaps it would not have done us so much harm.'

I agreed, naturally. He turned into a small child, and in that ward, among twenty-three other patients, unrestrained and unashamed, he cried bitterly.

Morris had a long spell of good days after this. He started a friendship with a female visitor. He was on the best of terms with the ward and keenly interested in all that was going on.

On one of my visits he asked me how long he had been in the hospital now.

When I told him, he said, 'Three months, and I have not had a single fury since being here. How much do you think this is worth?' he wanted to know.

I said I did not know. How much was it?

'You can't express it in gold, it is too much, it is everything,' he said.

On another occasion he said, 'I feel very small here. Do you understand what I mean?'

'No, I don't.'

'It is like this; when they tell me here that I should stop playing the gramophone, I stop. And when they want their silly music, I play their silly music for them. I think; let them, they want it, they are also ill. I am not demanding here. In the nursing home it was different. I wanted milk all the time, do you remember? I always thought that they did not give me enough. That I had the right to have more. Here I do not feel like that. Funny that I can see now, that it was all in my mind. I could not see it then. One cannot see it while one is in such trouble.'

Two days later he heard that he had no chance to be sent to Switzerland as he had hoped. He reported this and said that when he was told about it, he thought he would go mad.

'And now?' I said.

He shrugged his shoulders.

'We shall find out whether it is really impossible,' I said, convinced I had to try.

He replied, 'Does not exist, hundred per cent!'

'What do you mean?'

'Does not exist, hundred-per-cent-impossible. There are always possibilities.'

This was for all of them an unshakeable conviction. They knew about this.

For the next three days he suffered severely from indigestion. He wanted to explain, and said, 'Die alten zeiten brennen mich.' (The old days are burning me inside.)

In November 1947, a bed in the Jewish sanatorium in Devon was found for him and we both flew there. When he heard he would be together with former concentration camp inmates at this sanatorium he became frightened.

'What will I do if I start up my old ways again?'

He soon realized that his fears were unfounded. The atmosphere in the sanatorium and the behaviour of the other patients made him feel at ease. When we separated, he was calm and hopeful for his recovery. The doctors were not without hope for him either.

His fate is in the balance. It is not clear yet, whether he will, as the others have done, make a compromise and choose a very hard and painful life rather than death. His lung is very severely damaged, but his mind is improving. Perhaps he will, and perhaps he will not, be able to live. There is a rare pool of strength at his command, on which he can draw in his fight. He is clear in his mind about the issue, as is obvious from the following realistic and matter-of-fact response which he gave me when I asked permission to reproduce his story and give a report about his behaviour.

'Yes, you may,' he said. 'If I live, it will be interesting. If I die, it will be something of me which will still be there.'

That something should be there of them is the aim of this report. Who can reproduce all the facets of their personalities? Personalities that were changing so quickly? I knew only a few of them well. What I spoke about in the beginning, my reluctance to meet with them as individual people, had melted away in the process of our working together.

I am leaving them now, wondering what it really was that decided whether or not they could 'take' their trials. Perhaps those who were immature and less secure than others and therefore too young (as Morris had said of himself) could not stand it. It was the good homes which produced the survivors. The homes in which there had been sunshine and rain—enough love and the right number of demands, enough of both to give the child a climate in which it could best grow, supported by love, and learning by frustration, becoming acquainted with reality, content and satisfied with what it met, and looking out for more, in turn... and then I thought about how marvellously keen many of them were to see clearly. How direct and simple the mechanism within them started working towards sanity once it had the slightest chance of turning in that direction. Of course, they were young. And though that had been to their disadvantage in the past, perhaps it was to their advantage now. They were like a field, ploughed over in spring. Seeds would germinate well in that broken-up earth. And I felt the responsibility heavily which we had carried, who had been their first contacts in the new world.

I asked myself how much they had benefitted directly from the teaching, how much from the personal contact, how much from the fact that I had given them of my time and made every effort I possibly could to help them rearrange their situation, how far they would have advanced without it. I cannot assess.

In my description I have aimed to show what happened in our case, what tormented them, and how on the spur of the moment I tried to deal with the situation. I am sure there would have been many ways, but all would have shown how little was necessary, as their goodwill unfolded in all its beauty. You had to experience it to believe how easily the innate strength of their sane nature turned towards life.

I recently saw a few hundred of them again at a Hanukah party after a year's gap. What an improvement! And yet how much they still displayed the same astonishing directness, the wit and the kindness.

It was wonderful for me to meet them again, and it was also a great chance for me to learn more, to learn again, and to see their lives forming their own patterns; to get a glimpse of how interwoven all happenings are by the light of understanding the framework into which they all fitted; to see events fall into place by the sheer logic of reality.

Is it too much to imagine that what enabled me to find a better balance in the swinging of my own life's curve must have helped steady theirs as well?

There is a poem by the same boy whose verses are printed here and there among the text. It was a birthday present to a young girl he grew fond of. It is printed here in German Yiddish as he wrote it, but an attempt is made to translate the last verse because of the third line in it, which describes better than I could the very quality which made them what they were: a joy to meet.

Wir tuen Deinen Gebutstag gruessen,

Mit einer Freude, mit einem Gesang,

Vielleicht brachte Dir Traum einen suessen,

Liebe, Freude als Geschenk.

Leben sollst Du mit Glueck und Wohl

Es sollen sich erfuellen Bitten Deine,

Was Dein Herz verlangt und will,

Das wuensche ich Dir, Freundin Meine.

Dein Gesicht soll immer gluecklich sein,

Du sollst nicht wissen von einem Schmerze

Dein Herz soll immer bleiben fein,

Das wuensche ich Dir von ganzem Herze.

[May your face always be happy

May you not know any pain

May your heart always be fine

I wish you a whole heart]

Afterword

In the case of Marie Paneth, and the archives revealed at the US Library of Congress, there is a tantalising, emotionally moving, though possibly frustrating, glimpse into the art therapy work that she did with young Holocaust survivors in the mid 1940's. Paintings by the young people with whom she worked and who were under her guidance and tutelage have survived. These art works offer us a direct connection to the raw and visceral emotions being played out at the time, often on rudimentary scraps of paper. Post-war austerity still prevailed and materials were obviously at a premium.

I say "frustrating" because we know in her personal writings that she does occasionally refer to specific art works by children, but we also know that the actual paintings and drawings that she references in "*Rock the Cradle*" are not those that have survived and that are shown in this version of this book.

Those of us involved in the publication of "*Rock the Cradle*" thought long and hard about how to work around this conundrum, that we have art works but not those referenced directly by Marie in the book, and decided that those we do have access to ought to be included, and are representative of the work that she did with so many traumatised young people. These works deserve exposure, and they do add an essential visual presence to the book when, after all, Marie was a visual artist.

Inevitably in these matters one brings one's own history and reflections to bear. Although I am not a qualified Art Therapist, I can perhaps add some of my own insights to their resonance. These insights have been gleaned from the past fifteen years of working with, and becoming close to, many of the child survivors who came to Marie Paneth's "Reception Camp, Windermere". Though they are not the work of the artist themselves they still have much in common with them. They would all have travelled through the concentration camp system of Nazi German Occupied Europe and arrived in Britain after the war.

We know as many as twenty per cent of the total number of three hundred youngsters who came to Windermere in 1945 actually had some engagement with Marie's art studios on the now well-known Calgarth Estate. The challenges she faced in working with the youngsters is laid bare in "*Rock the Cradle*" and her observations both during the art classes, and also of the life and behaviour outside on the estate, remain invaluable.

Those child Holocaust survivors from Windermere that I knew well in their later years had little recollection of an Art Therapist at Calgarth Estate in the Lake District in 1945. The team of carers brought together in Windermere by the CBF (Central British Fund) to care for the children included psychiatric support, and Marie Paneth was part of that aspect of the recovery team.

It is worth mentioning that the relationship between many of the children and the psychiatrists was not without problems. To have survived the camps alone, and to have seen much and lost everything, had enormous implications for a young person's dealings with any form of authority, no matter how well meaning the intention. Marie faced the same challenge on occasion, and especially during this initial period of adjustment for the young people.

Although one of the child survivors in later years did look back fondly hen reflecting on setting out on a career as an artist painter, he could not for certain say it was Marie in Windermere who set him on the path. Others, incidentally, do recall being taught to speak English in Windermere by someone we suspect was Marie, but the final proof must remain as simple conjecture. The system at Calgarth Estate was to provide support for the children and this also necessitated the ability to be adaptable in the circumstances. The scenario that the carer team faced was unprecedented, as indeed it was for all the one thousand plus residents who were still living on the estate when the children arrived from Prague. Tolerance and understanding were key to this early period of rehabilitation.

The paintings that have survived, and not all are presented in the book, show a range of ages of children, from early years to older youngsters. I am loath to place too much interpretation on the art works themselves but we could presume that they were retained for a purpose. There are images of a classic child "tadpole" figure, and Marie has retained examples with and without eyes. The houses depicted do tend to be of a deep brown colour, some shown detached and behind a fence, while others are a row of such houses. I cannot but think of either the classic, red brick British working class terraced house through the eyes of a child, nor can I not think of the deep brown of Theresienstadt ghetto. It was Theresienstadt where the children who came to Windermere were liberated from, a ghetto with its own unique place in history and where artists, writers, composers, performers, were incarcerated along with so many others.

I was in Theresienstadt with a reunion party of survivors and their families, and I cannot begin to express or describe the impact it had on one or two of the survivors, some of whom were returning for the first time since their liberation and ultimate journey to Windermere. The memories and cruelties of those days was utterly overwhelming and the joy of liberation was, and always is, tempered by an overpowering sense of loss. That is one aspect of what the children's images brought to my mind.

There is a curious page of drawings of women's clothes that remind me of a different scenario from the liberation of Theresienstadt, and that was a dramatic retelling of an equally powerful story of liberation, though from a different and equally notorious camp.

A survivor of Ravensbruck liberated at Belsen told me a of a remarkable connection to the Windermere group. She heard, after liberation that a relative from her family had survived when she had lost hope of any being alive. She discovered that her brother was alive and in Windermere at the Reception Camp. When I met her she recalled to me her liberation in Belsen, and the efforts of "those young British boys" of the British Army who had liberated them.

She said that they had also helped in other ways, and remembered how some of these soldiers "on their days off had set out a picnic blanket on the ground with food, a record player, and danced with us when we felt well enough to dance. We must have looked a state but they made us feel human again, like women, and they gave us lipstick as well. Now that sounds silly, "why should they want lipstick?", but it was so important to us. We wanted to look nice and be valued again, our appearance mattered and they made us feel that we mattered". She ended by saying "Do you know that many of those young boys died from looking after us? That is just so sad, they caught the diseases around the camp, it is just so sad".

These paintings and drawings by children and young people are much more than they first appear to be and their worth is ultimately immeasurable because of who produced them, and a remarkable woman who was at their side.

Part 4

The Windermere Children

The following list of names, dates and places of birth, was part of a report discovered in the National Archives. The report was written by the Immigration Officer who was at Crosby on Eden airfield near Carlisle when the Jewish children arrived from Prague on 14th August 1945. From Crosby on Eden they were then taken to the Windermere Reception Camp in the Lake District where they were cared for by Marie Paneth and a dedicated group of carers and specialists.

Surname	Firstname	DOB	Place	Nationality
Adler	Wolfgang	11.8.1930	Berlin	German
Ajzen	Chaim	10.12.1930	Warsaw	Polish
Alexandrowicz	Lola	22.11.1930	Ostrowice	Polish
Auerbach	Judis	20.4.1942	Vienna	Austrian
Altermann	Izek	10.10.1930	Ożarów	Polish
Balsam	Hersch	15.8.1931	Gorlice	Polish
Balsam	Jadwiga	20.12.1932	Piotrkow	Polish
Banach	Jacob	10.10.1930	Brzesko Nove	Polish
Baumel	Moniek	6.1.1931	Demblin	Polish
Bayer	Jacob	15.6.1930	Siedlice	Polish
Beckermann	Paul	20.10.1930	Chmielnik	Polish
Beil	Abek	12.11.1931	Korsno	Polish
Berger	Felix	10.10.1930	Wlosceczowa	Polish
Berger	Josef	20.6.1933	Vienna	Austrian
Berlowitz	Asta	3.12.1930	Elbing	German
Berlowitz	Jacob	25.4.1931	Elbing	German
Berlowitz	Samuel	15.1.1934	Elbing	German
Bienstock	Benick	9.6.1932	Warsaw	Polish
Binke	Szlama	29.1.1931	Lodz	Polish
Blumenstein	Eiszel	1.1.1931	Piaseczno	Polish
Borenstein	Schmul	23.12.1931	Piotrkow	Polish
Borgenicht	David	4.7.1930	Krynica	Polish

Brand	Hirsch	5.8.1930	Ulacz	Polish
Brauner	Chiel	2.6.1932	Piotrkow	Polish
Braunheim	Salomon	28.8.1930	Frysztak	Polish
Breitberg	Salomon	27.7.1931	Kaminsk	Polish
Buergermann	Honick	30.10.1930	Lodz	Polish
Buki	Moniek	9.12.1931	Katowice	Polish
Bulka	Jakob	19.8.1930	Turek	Polish
Bumstueck	Mayer	28.12.1930	Staszow	Polish
Cederbaum	Josef	7.10.1930	Lodz	Polish
Cohnheim	Avigdor	29.4.1941	Berlin	German
Denderowicz	David	4.7.1930	Leopoldow	Polish
Dessau	Kopel	10.10.1930	Piotrkow	Polish
Diamant	Samuel	9.9.1931	Lodz	Polish
Dichter	Abraham	27.3.1932	Krubieszow	Polish
Dobrowolska	Mascha	11.11.1931	Bolchatow	Polish
Dresdner	Samuel	2.7.1930	Warsaw	Polish
Dzialowski	Feiwel	6.9.1930	Lodz	Polish
Ehrlich	Alfred	5.10.1930	Piotrkow	Polish
Ehrreich	Salomon	6.8.1930	Zmigrod	Polish
Ehrreich	Abraham	6.3.1930	Zmigrod	Polish
Eisenberg	Jakob	15.4.1931	Staszow	Polish
Elkenbaum	Abraham	26.12.1930	Pulawy	Polish
Englard	Benek	7.8.1932	Cracow	Polish
Esterreicher	Tilla	19.11.1930	Sosnovice	Polish
Etkind	Moses	2.10.1930	Lodz	Polish
Fajngesicht	Jankiel	10.12.1930	Ryki	Polish
Falinover	Salek	5.5.1930	Warsaw	Polish
Feiermann	Sala	14.8.1931	Lodz	Polish
Felsenfeld	Jsmael	2.8.39	Berlin	German
Fersra enig	Jsak	4.9.1930	Radom	Polish
Finkelstein	Szyja	19.12.1933	Piotrkow	Polish
Fisch	Jurek	15.12.1930	Bodzentin	Polish
Fischelberg	Chiel	9.12.1931	Brzesko	Polish
Folkart	Lydia	1.10.1930	Mor. Ostrova	Czech
Frank	Peter	28.12.1929	Praha	Czech
Freikorn	Mendel	15.7.1930	Szeseksein	Polish

Freimann	Salomon	1.9.1930	Jeziorna	Polish
Freimann	Salomon	7.10.1930	Piotrkow	Polish
Friedberg	Berek	8.10.1930	Deblin	Polish
Friedberg	Laib	6.6.1933	Deblin	Polish
Friedmann	Gerson	15.9.1930	Lodz	Polish
Friedmann	Israel	3.9.1930	Lodz	Polish
Friedmann	Nachman	15.8.1930	Zdunska Wola	Polish
Fruchtzweig	Moses	28.9.1930	Bendzin	Polish
Fuchs	Chaim	15.7.1931	Tuszyn	Polish
Fuchs	Jajna	2.9.1930	Tuszyn	Polish
Gastfreund	Israel	18.11.1930	Lodz	Polish
Glickson	Jacob	8.11.1930	Czenstochowa	Polish
Gold	Abraham	15.10.1930	Gorlice	Polish
Goldberg	Jan	4.8.1930	Bielsko	Polish
Goldberg	Josef	5.8.1930	Kozienice	Polish
Goldberg	Schmul	9.12.1930	Piotrkow	Polish
Goldberg	Szmul	25.11.1930	Bendzin	Polish
Golde	Henryk	5.5.1932	Plock	Polish
Goldcecker	Hersch	15.9.1930	Opatow	Polish
Goldhersz	Lola	20.7.1930	Piotrkow	Polish
Goldstein	Abraham	10.11.1930	Miedryszec	Polish
Grabbia	Abraham	22.12.1931	Breswzko-Nove	Polish
Graf	Henna	1.9.1930	Bratislava	Slovakia
Graf	Paul	16.3.1930	Bratislava	Slovakia
Gross	Franja	9.4.1931	Lodz	Polish
Grossmann	Isak	17.10.1930	Warzaw	Polish
Grossmann	Pinkus	8.9.1930	Strzemieszyce	Polish
Gruch	Henryk	15.7.1930	Strzemieszyce	Polish
Gruenbaum	Efraim	20.7.1931	Piotrkow	Polish
Gruenbaum	Guta	8.8.1930	Lodz	Polish
Gruener	Sylvia	17.2.1939	Vienna	Austria
Grunfeld	Otto	12.6.1930	Berlin	German
Grzmot	Motek	13.9.1930	Sosnovice	Polish
Gumener	Else	17.1.1931	Lodz	Polish
Gutter	Pinkus	21.7.1932	Lodz	Polish
Haase	Juergen	17.2.1936	Berlin	German

Halter	Roman	7.9.1930	Chodecz	Polish
Harringer	Peter	4.3.1934	Breslau	German
Hausmann	Rela	5.10.1930	Sieradz	Polish
Helfgott	Beer	20.12.1930	Vydava	Polish
Herschberg	Jerzy	18.8.1930	Poznan	Polish
Herschkowicz	David	13.9.1930	Jemdrzejow	Polish
Herschkowicz	Majer	30.9.1930	Sieradz	Polish
Herschlikowicz	Moniek	8.8.1930	Piotrkow	Polish
Herszlikowicz	Arek	13.9.1931	Sieradz	Polish
Himmelfarb	Wolf	19.6.1930	Kopszewica	Polish
Hirschfeld	David	15.8.1930	Gorlice	Polish
Hirschfeld	Moniek	15.8.1930	Gorlice	Polish
Hochmann	Martin	15.2.1930	Munkacevo	Polish
Hochspiegel	Sale	23.8.1930	Lodz	Polish
Hoffmann	Martin	15.2.1930	Praha	Czech
Holzkenner	Samuel	15.9.1930	Warzawa	Polish
Honigwachs	Michael	3.9.1929	Nowy Jicim	Czech
Hubermann	Abraham	28.12.1930	Warzawa	Polish
Husserl	Zdenka	6.2.1939		
Jacob	Agnes	3.9.1942	Debrecin	Polish
Jacob	Judith	10.1.1939	Debrecin	Polish
Jacob	Sultan	17.12.1936	Debrecin	Polish
Jacobowicz	Izek	24.7.1930	Lodz	Polish
Jacubowicz	Ala	18.6.1930	Lodz	Polish
Jacubowicz	Arman	3.4.1929	Uzmorod	Polish
Josef	Gad	22.10.1942	Berlin	German
Jonisch	David	9.8.1930	Serock	Polish
Judenschneider	Szlama	17.5.1933	Demblin	Polish
Judkewicz	Chaim	7.10.1930	Piotrkow	Polish
Kadisiewicz	Elias	4.4.1930	Starachovice	Polish
Kadzidlo	Moses	13.9.1930	Radomsk	Polish
Kalmowicz	Simon	26.2.1930	Kielce	Polish
Kamaryth	Ruth	28.2.1938	Vienna	Austria
Kaminski	Motel	15.6.1932	Piotrkow	Polish
Kamionka	Motek	5.6.1931	Warzawa	Polish
Kandelzucker	Kopel	11.10.1930	Bialoblzegi	Polish

Kirszberg	Abraham	16.7.1930		Polish
Kleinmann	Chemia	1.2.1932	Sandomierz	Polish
Klin	Simon	15.11.1930	Zdunska Wola	Polish
Kloc	Markus	26.9.1930	Frysztak	Polish
Kochen	Majer	10.9.1930	Kielce	Polish
Kohn	Chaim	10.10.1930	Smigrod Novy	Polish
Kohn	Estera	27.8.1930	Lodz	Polish
Kohn	Hans	24.12.1930	Berlin	German
Kohn	Josef	5.9.1930	Lodz	Polish
Kolasz	Israel	15.4.1930	Proszovice	Polish
Korman	Bluma	20.6.1933	Radom	Polish
Korman	Chaim	15.4.1931	Radom	Polish
Kornfeld	Bernhard	1.1.1930	Sandomericz	Polish
Koziwoda	Moniek	21.5.1931	Piotrkow	Polish
Krowiczky	Jacob	25.7.1932	Lodz	Polish
Kura	Jacob	4.8.1930	Kalisz	Polish
Kurncnz	Pinkus	15.3.1931	Piotrkow	Polish
Kurtz	Jan	5.4.1931	Cracow	Polish
Kuszer	Binem	11.1.1931	Piotrkow	Polish
Kuszermann	Rifka	18.3.1930	Radom	Polish
Kuszermann	Szlama	3.5.1931	Radom	Polish
Kuttner	David	25.4.1931	Konstantinov	Polish
Kuttner	Izek	24.11.1930	Lodz	Polish
Laskier	Schmul	27.8.1931	Warzawa	Polish
Lazarus	Berl	21.5.1942	Berlin	German
Lecker	Simon	15.12.1930	Rymanow	Polish
Lefkowicz	Chaim	21.10.1930	Piotrkow	Polish
Lenschner	Dadek	19.7.1931	Czenstechowa	Polish
Lewkowicz	Mordche	28.12.1930	Lodz	Polish
Lewkowicz	Perez	9.9.1930	Lodz	Polish
Lichtenberg	Samuel	26.7.1930	Lodz	Polish
Licht	Israel	4.1.1931	Lodz	Polish
Liebermann	Simche	10.12.1930	Warzawa	Polish
Loeffelholz	Salomon	22.10.1930	Krakow	Polish
Loewenstein	Motek	28.12.1930	Chmielnik	Polish
Lossau	Ingrid	16.5.1936	Koenigsberg	German

Lossau	Joachim	16.5.1936	Koenigsberg	German
Lossau	Max	22.11.1934	Koenigsberg	German
Lossau	Renate	19.10.1930	Koenigsberg	German
Lossau	Waltraut	19.1.1933	Koenigsberg	German
Malinicky	Moses	18.8.1930	Piotrkow	Polish
Markowiecki	Schmul	15.8.1930	Kielce	Polish
Melzer	Jaccob	10.5.1932	Warzaw	Polish
Mincberg	Fraim	15.11.1930	Zdunska Wola	Polish
Mlinczkiewicz	Majer	22.3.1932	Demblin	Polish
Mlynarski	Hersch	15.8.1930	Piotrkow	Polish
Morgenstern	Abraham	27.1.1932	Lodz	Polish
Moncasz	Jacob	13.12.1932	Suchedniow	Polish
Muench	Denny	2.1.1940	Cologne	German
Muench	Tena	23.9.1939	Berlin	German
Munter	Mina	1.12.1930	Warta	Polish
Neumann	Morschek	1.8.1930	Wierzbnik	Polish
Neumark	Josef	28.8.1930	Praszka	Polish
Neustaedter	Benek	22.12.1930	Skarzysko	Polish
Niessenbaum	Bronislaw	24.3.1931	Warzaw	Polish
Nurtmann	Mosche	1.8.1930	Warta	Polish
Obuchovski	Berek	28.12.1930	Alexandrov	Polish
Orenstein	Salek	10.11.1930	Opatov	Polish
Orzech	Chaskel	20.8.1930	Kielce	Polish
Orzech	Rubin	20.8.1930	Kielce	Polish
Pantoffalmacher	Solomon	15.7.1931	Nasielsk	Polish
Pawlowski	Abraham	17.10.1932	Lodz	Polish
Perlmutter	Mayer	21.10.1930	Opatow	Polish
Peter	Mendel	7.10.1930	Radzin	Polish
Pomeranz	Issaak	2.9.1930	Dzialoszyce	Polish
Popiel	Schmul	7.10.1930	Gorlice	Polish
Posnanski	Arthur	7.11.1930	Prazka	Polish
Posnanski	Jerszy	22.5.1932	Prazka	Polish
Przendza	Jurek	11.9.1930	Dzialoszyce	Polish
Rafael	Margot	3.9.1935	Berlin	German
Radzynski	Kopel	9.1.1933	Bendzin	Polish
Ratz	Josef	29.9.1930	Rzeszow	Polish

Reiber	Baruch	3.4.1931	Klobucko	Polish
Reichkind	Moniek	15.6.1931	Lodz	Polish
Reizmann	Alexander	15.11.1930	Lodz	Polish
Reichmann	Isak	15.11.1930	Lodz	Polish
Richter	Leiser	15.11.1930	Plzytik Naz	Polish
Richter	Rela	15.5.1930	Przytyk	Polish
Rosen	Katharine	14.8.1930	Vienna	Austrian
Rosenbaum	Brigitte	15.12.1932	Eisenstadt	German
Rosenbaum	Moniek	20.5.1931	Gorlice	Polish
Rosenberg	Abraham	1.8.1930	Sosnovice	Polish
Rosenberg	Leon	27.12.1930	Ostrovice	Polish
Rosenberg	Moses	28.2.1931	Cracow	Polish
Rosenblatt	Hermann	30.9.1930	Pruszez	Polish
Rosenblatt	Selig	25.7.1930	Warsaw	Polish
Rosenblum	Chaskel	5.10.1930	Konskie	Polish
Rosengarten	Samuel	8.8.1930	Krakow	Polish
Rosenthal	Bella	17.8.1942	Berlin	German
Rosenzweig	Naftali	15.11.1930	Ksiencz Wielki	Polish
Rowelski	Gittel	23.4.1932	Berlin	German
Rozagara	Henryk	25.10.1930	Warsaw	Polish
Rudzinski	Israel	15.11.1930	Piotrkow	Polish
Sachs	Henrik	1.5.1931	Czenstoshowa	Polish
Saks	Simon	15.7.1933	Bendzin	Polish
Salomon	Abraham	12.12.1930	Dzialoszyce	Polish
Samel	Hirsch	15.10.1932	Piotrokow	Polish
Schindler	Alfred	23.6.1931	Kettbus	Polish
Schindler	Max	18.12.1930	Kettbus	Polish
Schnitzer	Josef	31.7.1931	Leipzig	German
Schonberger	Elias	23.7.1930	Suchy	Polish
Schottland	Moniek	4.4.1930	Lodz	Polish
Schulsinger	Abraham	14.11.1930	Melnik	Polish
Schwach	Kamilla	12.6.1932	Vienna	Austrian
Schwarz	Emil	7.3.1930	Munkasz	Russian
Szurek	Dan	10.7.1931	Lodz	Polish
Szhwarz	Abraham	3.10.1931	Tuszyn	Polish
Schweizer	Bella	15.3.1931	Lodz	Polish

Schwimmer	Wisha	5.5.1931	Gorlitzer	Polish
Senkpiel	Gisela	3.3.1931	Kiel	German
Silberger	Julek	27.10.1931	Lodz	Polish
Silberschatz	Adolf	7.12.1930	Lodz	Polish
Silberstein	Mendel	8.7.1930	Lodz	Polish
Singer	Judith	17.2.1940	Vienna	Austrian
Siegelfarb	Jehoschua	24.12.1930	Lodz	Polish
Semner	David	30.11.1930	Turek	Polish
Sonnenschein	Feige	25.5.1939	Vienna	Austrian
Sosnowicz	Meyer	13.6.1930	Warsaw	Polish
Spiegel	Jona	18.12.1941	Vionza	Austrian
Spier	Ruth	15.10.1930	Berlin	German
Spire	Chaim	21.9.1930	Piotzkow	Polish
Szlamberg	Chaim	31.12.1930	Lodz	Polish
Szleinsicht	Cesia	25.5.1931	Demblin	Polish
Szleinsicht	Moniek	18.10.1932	Demblin	Polish
Szleinsicht	Roman	15.3.1930	Demblin	Polish
Steinbrecher	Emil	10.3.1932	Bendzin	Polish
Steinmann	Leon	10.4.1931	Ostrowico	Polish
Sternfeld	Mieteck	3.9.1930	Zgicrz	Polish
Stebierki	Jakob	4.12.1930	Wielun	Polish
Strauss	Renate	12.3.1930	Ungrer	N/A
Tebacznik	Meritz	7.5.1930	Demblin	Polish
Tarke	Jaine	10.8.1930	Talkow	Polish
Tennebaum	Selig	7.12.1930	Kozienice	Polish
Tepper	Lipa	30.11.1930	Dukla	Polish
Trzebinier	Salomon	5.8.1930	Piotrkow	Polish
Tuch	Horitz	9.5.1931	Wielun	Polish
Turek	Rosa	10.7.1930	Sosnowiec	Polish
Unger	Anita	16.6.1935	Lodz	Polish
Verstand	Jakob	10.8.1932	Kozenice	Polish
Wagstock	Marian	5.7.1930	Klodawa	Polish
Wagszal	Loib	29.8.1930	Frysztck	Polish
Wald	Nathan	8.12.1930	Grudziadz	Polish
Warszniter	Hersch	19.7.1931	Lodz	Polish
Wasserzicher	Rolf	20.9.1931	Lodz	Polish

Wegner	Harry	20.10.1930	Koenigsberg	German
Weichhaendler	Chaim	5.7.1932	Starachovice	Polish
Weichhaendler	Hersch	23.11.1930	Starachovice	Polish
Weinberg	Felix	2.4.1928	Aussig	Czech
Weinryt	Henryk	13.6.1933	Czenstechowa	Polish
Weismann	Izek	9.7.1931	Starachovice	Polish
Weissbaum	Israel	7.6.1930	Piotrkow	Polish
Weizenblueth	Sewek	27.11.1930	Warsaw	Polish
Werthmann	Abraham	5.12.1930	Gora Kalvaria	Polish
Wiernik	David	21.6.1931	Lodz	Polish
Wierzbicki	Mayer	5.12.1930	Warsaw	Polish
Wilder	Israel	3.12.1932	Piotrkow	Polish
Winogrodzki	Rafael	7.3.1930	Piotrkow	Polish
Wolfcwiecz	Benek	3.3.1931	Szydlowice	N/A
Wolkowicz	Stefa	4.12.1935	Lodz	Polish
Wolreich	Abraham	2.5.1931	Piotrkow	Polish
Wurzel	Berek	28.5.1932	Radom	Polish
Wurzel	Bluma	2.8.1930	Radomsko	Polish
Wrebel	Peter	17.2.1935	Munich	German
Zahler	Elfriede	7.9.1936	Vienna	Austrian
Zeligfeld	Moszek	10.10.1930	Krakow	Polish
Zielgler	Hanna	2.2.1931	Piotrkow	Polish
Zweigenbaum	Szlama	14.2.1933	Bendzin	Polish
Zwirek	Abraham	19.12.1930	Plock	Polish
Zylberger	Porez	13.12.1930	Lodz	Polish
Zyskind	Hersch	10.6.1931	Piotrkow	Polish

My late father, Moishe Malenicky was born in a small town called Piotrkow in Poland.

His mother was Chana, his father Elimelech and they were bakers. My dad was the eldest of six children. He had a younger brother Nathan and four little sisters, Surela, Frumka, Perla and the youngest Miriam, who was seven when the Nazis invaded.

His entire family were murdered in the gas chambers of Treblinka concentration camp. In 1942 The Nazi killing machine massacred, in this camp alone, 10,000 men, woman and children every single day.

My dad was the only survivor of his entire family. He was liberated from Theresienstadt, just outside Prague.

In August 1945 my father was one of the three hundred children to arrive in Windermere, in the Lake District. They really thought they had arrived in Paradise.

Marie Paneth's account of her time with this young group makes for a fascinating read! She realised that these children who had witnessed and somehow survived the most heinous period in modern history had to somehow continue their lives and find happiness.

As a one of the second generation, Marie's diary is an insight into the work and commitment that was made to help rebuild my dad's life.

Angela Cohen

2ND GENERATION
PUBLISHING